Raising Resilient Families

Practical advice, psychological insights, and actionable strategies to foster healthy and resilient family environments.

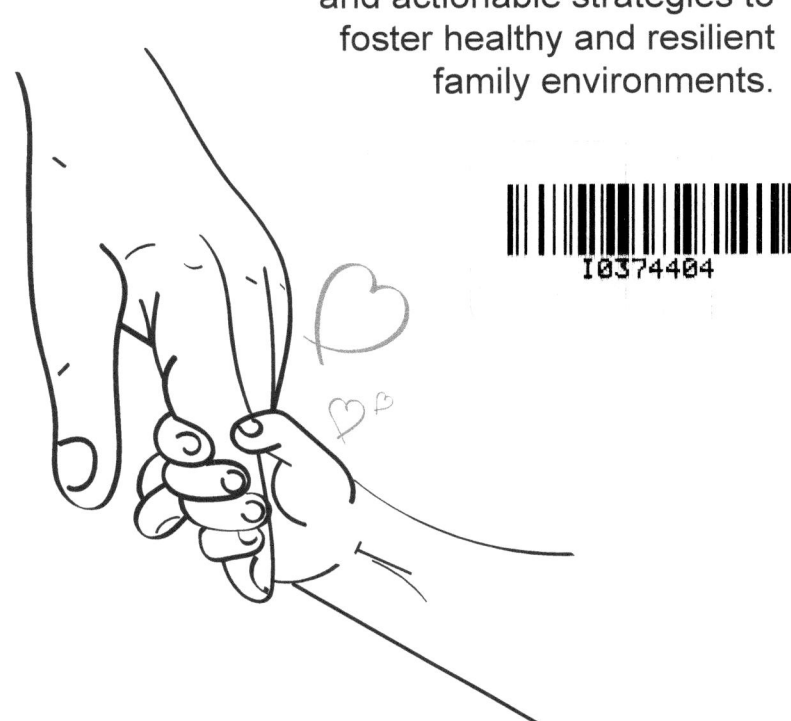

Deborah Sugirthakumar

First published by Busybird Publishing 2024

Copyright © 2024 Deborah Sugirthakumar

ISBN:
Paperback: 978-1-923216-61-7
Ebook: 978-1-923216-62-4

This work is copyright. Apart from any use permitted under the *Copyright Act 1968*, no part of this publication may be reproduced, stored in a retrieval system or transmitted in any form or by any means, electronic, mechanical, photocopying, recording or otherwise, without the prior written permission of Deborah Sugirthakumar.

The information in this book is based on the author's experiences and opinions. The author and publisher disclaim responsibility for any adverse consequences, which may result from use of the information contained herein. Permission to use any external content has been sought by the author. Any breaches will be rectified in further editions of the book.

Cover Image: Busybird Publishing

Cover design: Busybird Publishing

Layout and typesetting: Busybird Publishing

Busybird Publishing
2/118 Para Road
Montmorency, Victoria
Australia 3094
www.busybird.com.au

I want to begin by expressing my deepest gratitude to my extraordinary parents. Your unwavering love, guidance and strength have been the bedrock of my life, especially during my most challenging moments. To my sister and brother-in-law, your support has been a comforting embrace, reminding me that I'm never alone on this journey.

To my extended family, friends and colleagues, thank you for your constant encouragement and belief in me. Each word of support has lifted my spirits and fuelled my determination.

Lastly, I dedicate this book to my beloved son, Daronn. You are my light, my purpose and my greatest source of inspiration. Everything I do is for you, and I hope to instil in you the same strength and love that has shaped my life.

You are my heart.

May boys grow wise, with hearts that feel,
empowered to seek when life won't heal.
May girls grow safe, in love's embrace,
a world where kindness fills the space.
Let's end the violence, break the chain,
and build a world free from pain.
Together, strong, resilient, free;
a safer, kinder society we shall be.

Contents

CHAPTER 1
UNDERSTANDING FAMILY VIOLENCE AND ITS IMPACT ON FAMILIES — 1

CHAPTER 2
THE FOUNDATION OF A SAFE AND LOVING HOME — 6

CHAPTER 3
TEACHING EMPATHY AND COMPASSION — 12

CHAPTER 4
BUILDING EMOTIONAL INTELLIGENCE IN CHILDREN — 18

CHAPTER 5
INSTILLING RESPECT FOR SELF AND OTHERS — 24

CHAPTER 6
ENCOURAGING RESPONSIBILITY AND ACCOUNTABILITY — 30

CHAPTER 7
FOSTERING POSITIVE TRAITS IN BOYS — 36

CHAPTER 8
EMPOWERING GIRLS TO STAND UP FOR THEMSELVES' — 43

CHAPTER 9
PROMOTING HEALTHY COMMUNICATION SKILLS — 50

CHAPTER 10
TEACHING CONFLICT RESOLUTION AND PROBLEM-SOLVING SKILLS — 57

CHAPTER 11
DEVELOPING RESILIENCE IN CHILDREN — 64

CHAPTER 12
THE POWER OF POSITIVE REINFORCEMENT — 70

CHAPTER 13
THE ROLE OF COMMUNITY AND SUPPORT NETWORKS — 76

CHAPTER 14
HEALING FROM THE PAST AND MOVING FORWARD — 82

CHAPTER 15
CREATING A LEGACY OF LOVE AND RESPECT   89

CHAPTER 16
THE ROLE OF COMMUNITIES IN SUPPORTING PARENTS
AND RAISING RESILIENT CHILDREN   95

CHAPTER 17
GOVERNMENT'S ROLE IN SUPPORTING FAMILIES AND
ERADICATING FAMILY VIOLENCE   99

Helplines and Support Services (Australia)   105

Epilogue   107

References   109

Acknowledgements   111

About the Author   113

Disclaimer

This book addresses sensitive topics related to family violence and its impact on individuals and families. The content within these pages is intended to raise awareness, provide insights and offer guidance on fostering resilience and positive traits in children to prevent violence in the future.

Readers are advised that some material may be triggering or distressing. If you or someone you know is currently experiencing family violence or any form of abuse, I strongly encourage you to seek professional help immediately. Resources and support are available through national and local helplines, counselling services and emergency assistance.

The information provided in this book is for educational purposes and should not replace the advice of health professionals or legal counsel. The author and publisher are not responsible for any adverse effects or consequences resulting from the use of or reliance on any information contained in this book.

CHAPTER 1

UNDERSTANDING FAMILY VIOLENCE AND ITS IMPACT ON FAMILIES

'Violence against women is perhaps the most shameful human rights violation. And it is perhaps the most pervasive. It knows no boundaries of geography, culture or wealth.'

– Kofi Annan, former UN Secretary-General

Family violence is an insidious force that infiltrates the home, shattering the very foundation of safety, trust and love that families rely on to thrive. It is not limited to physical abuse; rather, it encompasses a range of behaviours designed to exert power and control over another person. These behaviours can include emotional manipulation, verbal degradation, financial restriction, sexual coercion and psychological intimidation. Family violence is a pattern of behaviour, not an isolated incident, and its impact reverberates far beyond the individuals directly involved; it ripples out to affect entire families and communities.

The forms of family violence vary widely, but they all share a common goal: to dominate and diminish the victim. Physical violence, such as hitting, slapping or choking, is often the most visible form, but it is just the tip of the iceberg. Emotional abuse, which might involve constant criticism, belittling and humiliation, can leave deeper scars that are not visible to the naked eye. Verbal abuse, filled with threats and insults, erodes a person's sense of self-worth. Financial abuse, where one partner controls all the money and limits the other's access to resources, strips away independence and creates a debilitating dependence. Sexual abuse, whether through forced intercourse or manipulation, violates the most intimate boundaries of a person, leaving behind profound trauma. Each of these forms of abuse can occur in isolation or, more commonly, in combination, creating a toxic environment that is as suffocating as it is destructive.

According to the World Health Organisation (WHO) family violence remains a global crisis with approximately 1 in 3 women worldwide experiencing either physical or sexual violence, predominantly by an intimate partner. The WHO highlights the severe long-term effects on mental, physical and reproductive health, stating that family violence is not only a violation of human rights but a public health crisis. It impacts entire communities by destabilising family units and perpetuating cycles of abuse that can transcend generations. Research also shows that children who witness family violence are at higher risk of developing emotional, behavioural and psychological issues, with long-term impacts on their well-being and development.

At the heart of family violence lies a cycle of abuse that is both predictable and devastating. This cycle typically follows a pattern: tension builds, an abusive incident occurs, the abuser apologies or makes excuses and a temporary calm is restored before the tension begins to build again. The cycle may start slowly, with long periods of calm between incidents, but over time, the frequency and severity of the abuse tend to escalate. This cycle creates a confusing and terrifying environment for victims, who may feel trapped, hopeless and unsure of how to break free.

Children who grow up in homes where family violence is present are deeply affected, even if they are not directly targeted by the abuse. They may witness the violence, hear the screams or sense the tension, leaving them in a state of constant anxiety. The effects on children can be profound and long lasting. Some children may become withdrawn and fearful, while others might act out in aggression, mirroring the behaviour they see at home. The trauma of living in a violent household can affect their emotional development, leading to issues with trust, self-esteem and relationships later in life.

The impact of family violence on children extends beyond the immediate emotional toll. Children who witness or experience family violence are at greater risk for developing mental health issues, including anxiety, depression and post-traumatic stress disorder (PTSD). They may struggle in school, have difficulty forming healthy relationships and, tragically, some may go on to repeat the cycle of violence in their own adult relationships. The trauma they experience can disrupt their sense of safety and stability, undermining their ability to build resilience, the very quality that helps individuals and families cope with adversity.

Family resilience is the ability of a family to withstand and recover from challenges, maintaining a sense of cohesion, support and positive identity despite difficulties. Family violence, however, erodes this resilience. When one family member uses fear and control to dominate others, it destroys the trust and unity that are essential for resilience. The family becomes fractured, with individuals isolated from each other emotionally, if not physically. The supportive bonds that should provide strength in times of hardship are instead replaced by fear and mistrust. In such an environment, it becomes nearly impossible for the family to function as a cohesive unit, and the effects are felt by all members, particularly children.

Breaking the cycle of family violence is not just essential for the well-being of those directly involved; it is crucial for future generations who might otherwise inherit the same patterns of behaviour. Children who grow up in abusive households may come to see violence as a normal part of relationships. Without intervention, they are at risk of becoming either perpetrators or victims of abuse in their own adult lives. However, when the cycle is broken, when a victim finds the safety they need to leave, when they access support and begin the process of healing, there is hope. With the right tools and support, children can learn that violence is not a solution, that love does not hurt and that they have the power to create a different, healthier future for themselves and their families.

The importance of breaking this cycle cannot be overstated. It requires more than just removing oneself from an abusive situation; it demands a complete redefinition of what a healthy relationship looks like. It involves educating children and adults alike about respect, boundaries, communication and empathy. It means creating environments where people feel safe to seek help without fear of judgment or retaliation. And, most importantly, it means fostering a culture where violence is not tolerated in any form, where every individual is valued and respected and where the sanctity of the home as a place of peace and love is fiercely protected.

Family violence is a pervasive issue that not only destroys individual lives but also undermines the very fabric of family resilience. Understanding its many forms, recognising the cycle of abuse and acknowledging its devastating impact on children are the first steps towards addressing this issue. By breaking the cycle of violence, we can help build stronger, more resilient families and ensure that future generations are not condemned to repeat the mistakes of the past. The journey may be difficult, but it is a necessary one – because every person deserves to live in a home free from fear, and every child deserves to grow up in a family that is safe, supportive and strong.

As a mother, I am deeply committed to raising my son with positive values that emphasise respect, empathy and emotional intelligence. From an early age, I teach him about the importance of boundaries, kindness and understanding the emotions of others. I make a conscious effort to foster an open environment where he feels safe to express his feelings, while also helping him to understand that power should never be used to harm others. Through stories, role-play and conversations, I instil in him the idea that true strength lies in compassion and respect for all individuals. For instance, when we discuss conflicts or emotions, I guide him to find peaceful resolutions and recognise the impact his actions may have on others. My aim is to ensure that he grows up understanding that healthy relationships are built on mutual trust and care, and that violence in any form is never acceptable.

By guiding him with these principles, I hope to break the cycle of violence and help shape a future generation of men who will contribute to creating safe, loving and respectful environments for everyone.

CHAPTER 2

THE FOUNDATION OF A SAFE AND LOVING HOME

'Children are not things to be moulded but are people to be unfolded.'

– Jess Lair, author and psychologist

The foundation of a safe and loving home is built on the bedrock of love, respect and safety. These elements are essential for creating an environment where each family member can thrive, especially children, who rely on the stability and security of their home as they grow and develop. In this chapter, we will explore how to establish such a home, emphasising the crucial role parents play as role models, the importance of building trust and open communication, and why emotional security is the cornerstone of a child's well-being.

Research from the Harvard Centre on the Developing Child (2015) emphasises that a child's early environment, particularly the home, plays a critical role in their emotional and cognitive development. A stable, loving and nurturing environment is essential for healthy brain development and for building a child's capacity for resilience. The report highlights that children who grow up in secure, emotionally supportive homes are more likely to develop healthy relationships, exhibit positive behaviour and cope better with stress as they grow. Conversely, a lack of emotional security or exposure to conflict and instability can lead to long-term negative outcomes, including anxiety, depression and difficulty forming trusting relationships in adulthood. Building a home where love and respect are prioritised lays the groundwork for a child's future success and emotional health.

Creating an Environment of Love, Respect and Safety

A home should be a sanctuary, a place where everyone feels cherished, valued and secure. Creating such an environment begins with love, which is the most powerful force in a family. Love is not just an emotion but an action, demonstrated through kindness, patience and understanding. It is shown in the way parents listen to their children, how they respond to their needs and the consistency with which they offer support and encouragement.

Respect is another critical component. It means acknowledging each person's individuality, treating each other with dignity and recognising that everyone in the family has rights and feelings that must be honoured. Respect fosters a sense of equality and fairness, which is essential for healthy family dynamics. It ensures that all family members, regardless of age or role, are given the space to express themselves without fear of judgment or dismissal.

Safety, both physical and emotional, is the final pillar. A safe home is one where children are protected from harm, whether that harm comes from outside threats or from within the family. Physical safety involves safeguarding children from accidents and dangers in their environment, while emotional safety requires shielding them from harsh words, criticism and actions that could damage their self-esteem. When a home is safe, children can explore, learn and grow without the constant fear of being hurt or belittled.

The Role of Parents as Role Models

Parents are the architects of the home environment, and their behaviour sets the tone for the entire household. Children learn not just from what their parents say but from what they do. This makes parents the most influential role model in a child's life. The way parents treat each other, how they handle stress, how they communicate and how they show love all serve as blueprints for their children's own behaviour.

To be effective role models, parents must embody the values they wish to instil in their children. If respect is a cornerstone of the family, parents must show respect in their interactions with each other and with their children. If kindness is valued, parents should practice patience and empathy, even in challenging situations. When children see their parents resolving conflicts peacefully, managing their emotions healthily and supporting each other, they learn to replicate these behaviours in their own lives.

Parents also need to be mindful of the messages they send, both intentionally and unintentionally. Children are incredibly perceptive and will pick up on inconsistencies between what is said and what is done. For example, if a parent tells a child to be honest but then lies in front of them, the child receives mixed signals about the value of honesty. Consistency between words and actions is crucial in reinforcing the values parents wish to impart.

Establishing Trust and Open Communication

Trust is the cornerstone of any healthy relationship, and this is especially true within a family. Trust is built over time through consistent, reliable behaviour. When children know they can depend on their parents to be there for them, to listen without judgment and to protect their interests, they develop a deep sense of trust that forms the basis of their relationship with their parents.

Open communication is a vital component of trust. Children need to feel that they can talk to their parents about anything, whether it's their hopes, fears, successes or struggles. This means creating an environment where dialogue is encouraged and where children are not afraid to express themselves. Active listening is key. Parents should give their full attention when their children speak, validate their feelings and respond thoughtfully.

It's also important for parents to share their own thoughts and feelings with their children, in an age-appropriate way. This openness helps children understand that their parents are also human beings with emotions and challenges, which can strengthen the parent–child bond. Moreover, it models healthy communication practices that children can use in their own relationships.

Establishing trust and open communication early on lays the groundwork for a strong, enduring relationship between parents and children. It ensures that when challenges arise, children feel comfortable turning to their parents for guidance and support.

The Importance of Emotional Security for Children

Emotional security is the bedrock upon which all other aspects of a child's development rest. When children feel emotionally secure, they have the confidence to explore the world, try new things and take risks. They know that they have a safe haven to return to, where they will be met with unconditional love and support.

Emotional security comes from knowing that they are loved for who they are, not for what they achieve. It means feeling accepted, even when they make mistakes or fall short of expectations. Parents play a crucial role in providing this security by offering consistent affection, encouragement and understanding. This doesn't mean shielding children from all challenges or discomforts, but rather providing them with the emotional tools to navigate life's ups and downs.

Children who grow up with emotional security are more likely to develop resilience, the ability to bounce back from setbacks and face adversity with strength. They are better equipped to form healthy relationships, as they have learned the importance of trust, respect and communication from their own family experiences. Moreover, emotionally secure children are less likely to engage in destructive behaviours, as they have a strong sense of self-worth and know they are valued.

The foundation of a safe and loving home is critical to the well-being and development of children. By creating an environment grounded in love, respect and safety, parents can foster a sense of security that allows their children to grow into confident, resilient individuals. Through their actions, parents serve as powerful role models, teaching their children the values that will guide them throughout their lives. Trust and open communication further strengthen the family bond, ensuring that children always feel supported and understood. Above all, emotional security gives children the confidence to face the world, knowing they have a solid foundation to rely on.

In building a safe and loving home for my son, I focus on creating an environment where he feels secure, valued and loved every day. Our home is a place where we emphasise trust, and I make it a priority to always keep the lines of communication open, encouraging him to share his thoughts and feelings without fear of judgment.

I also model the behaviour I want to instil in him. I treat others with kindness and respect, and I make sure that he sees healthy conflict resolution in action. By doing so, I hope to show him that disagreements can be resolved peacefully, and that love is always at the core of our interactions. In moments of discipline, I prioritise understanding over punishment, helping him understand why certain behaviours are unacceptable while reaffirming my love for him.

By making our home a safe and nurturing space, I aim to give him the emotional security that will enable him to grow into a compassionate, confident and resilient individual, equipped to form strong, loving relationships of his own.

CHAPTER 3

TEACHING EMPATHY AND COMPASSION

'Compassion is the basis of morality.'

– Arthur Schopenhauer, philosopher

Peaceful societies and loving homes have two things in common: empathy and compassion. These qualities help prevent violence, foster understanding and build stronger, more resilient relationships. As parents and caregivers, teaching empathy and compassion to children is one of the most powerful ways to shape a kinder, more harmonious world. In this chapter, we will explore what empathy is, why it is crucial for preventing violence, practical strategies for teaching it to children and how fostering these traits can lead to stronger family bonds.

Studies conducted by Paul Ekman (2003), a leading psychologist in the field of emotions, show that empathy is not only a learned behaviour but also a crucial skill for navigating social situations and building emotional intelligence. According to Ekman's research, empathy helps children recognise and understand the emotions of others, fostering better communication and reducing aggression. Children who are taught to practice empathy from an early age are more likely to develop positive social behaviours, such as sharing, helping and cooperating with others. Additionally, fostering empathy at home contributes to reducing instances of bullying, violence and antisocial behaviour, ultimately leading to a more compassionate society.

Understanding Empathy and Its Importance in Preventing Violence

Empathy is the ability to understand and share the feelings of another person. It involves not just recognising someone else's emotions but also imagining what it would be like to experience those emotions oneself. Compassion, a closely related concept, is the desire to help others when they are suffering. Together, empathy and compassion form the basis of caring relationships and moral behaviour.

The role of empathy in preventing violence cannot be understated. When individuals can empathise with others, they are less likely to cause harm because they understand the pain and suffering their actions could inflict. Empathy helps people to see beyond their own needs and desires, considering the impact of their behaviour on those around them. This understanding is crucial in breaking the cycle of violence that can permeate families and communities.

Without empathy, children may struggle to recognise the emotions of others, leading to misunderstandings, conflicts and, in extreme cases, acts of aggression or violence. By teaching empathy, parents can equip their children with the tools they need to navigate social interactions more thoughtfully, reducing the likelihood of harmful behaviours and fostering a more peaceful and cooperative environment.

Practical Ways to Teach Empathy to Children

Teaching empathy begins with modelling empathetic behaviour. Children learn by observing the actions of the adults around them, so parents and caregivers must demonstrate empathy in their daily interactions. When a child sees their parent showing concern for others, whether it's helping a neighbour in need or comforting a friend who is upset, they begin to understand the importance of being attuned to others' emotions.

Here are some practical strategies for teaching empathy to children:

Encourage Perspective-Taking

Help children understand how others might feel in different situations. When they see someone who is sad or upset, ask them to imagine how that person might be feeling and why. For example, after watching a movie or reading a story, discuss the characters' emotions and what might have caused them. This exercise helps children develop the ability to see the world from another's point of view.

Validate Emotions

Teach children that all emotions are valid and important. When a child expresses their feelings, acknowledge them and discuss why they feel that way. For instance, if your child is upset because a friend was mean to them, talk about how that experience made them feel and what might have caused their friend to act that way. This helps children understand that emotions are a natural response to life's challenges and that it's okay to talk about them.

Practice Active Listening

Show children the value of listening carefully to others. When someone is speaking, encourage your child to listen without interrupting, and then respond thoughtfully. This teaches them to respect others' feelings and opinions, even when they might not agree.

Use Role-Playing

Engage in role-playing exercises where children can act out different scenarios that require empathy. For example, pretend to be someone who has lost a toy and ask your child how they would feel and what they would do to help. Role-playing allows children to experiment with different emotions and responses in a safe environment.

Promote Helping Behaviours

Provide opportunities for your child to help others. This could be as simple as sharing toys with a sibling, helping with household chores or participating in community service activities. Acts of kindness, no matter how small, reinforce the value of caring for others and build a habit of compassionate behaviour.

Encouraging Kindness, Understanding and Compassion in Everyday Interactions

Empathy is best taught through everyday interactions. As parents, it's important to seize daily opportunities to encourage kindness, understanding and compassion. Here are some ways to weave these values into your family's daily routine:

Praise Kind Actions

When your child shows kindness, acknowledge and praise their behaviour. This positive reinforcement helps them associate good feelings with acts of compassion. For instance, if they share their snack with a friend, let them know how proud you are of their generosity.

Discuss the Impact of Actions

After conflicts or misunderstandings, talk with your child about how their actions might have affected others. Encourage them to think about what they could do differently next time to be more considerate.

Model Empathy in Conflict Resolution

When disagreements arise within the family, use them as teaching moments. Show your child how to resolve conflicts by considering everyone's feelings and finding solutions that respect those feelings. This not only teaches empathy but also equips them with problem-solving skills.

Create a Culture of Compassion

Make compassion a family value by engaging in activities that promote it. This could include volunteering together, supporting charitable causes or simply being there for each other during difficult times. When compassion is a core part of family life, it becomes a natural part of your child's behaviour.

How Empathy Helps Build Stronger, More Resilient Relationships

Empathy is a powerful force in building stronger, more resilient relationships. When children learn to understand and care for the feelings of others, they are better able to form meaningful, supportive connections. These relationships, in turn, become a source of strength and comfort throughout their lives.

Empathetic children are more likely to be good friends, siblings and, eventually, partners and parents. They are equipped to handle conflicts with understanding and are more willing to compromise and cooperate. This reduces the likelihood of strained or broken relationships and promotes harmony within the family and community.

Moreover, empathy fosters emotional intelligence, which is crucial for navigating the complexities of human interactions. Children who develop empathy are better at managing their emotions, understanding social cues and responding to the needs of others. This emotional intelligence helps them build deeper connections and creates a strong support network that can withstand life's challenges.

Teaching empathy and compassion is one of the most important responsibilities parents have. These qualities are not just about preventing negative behaviours; they are about creating a positive, nurturing environment where children can grow into kind, understanding and resilient individuals. By modelling empathetic behaviour, encouraging perspective-taking and fostering a culture of kindness in everyday interactions, parents can help their children develop the empathy and compassion needed to build strong, healthy relationships. These skills will serve them throughout their lives, enabling them to contribute to a more peaceful and caring world.

> In my journey of raising my son, teaching him empathy and compassion is something I prioritise every day. I believe that empathy starts at home, so I make a conscious effort to model these behaviours in my own interactions with others. When we encounter situations where someone might be struggling, such as seeing a homeless person or witnessing a classmate feeling left out, I use these as teaching moments. I encourage my son to think about how others feel and to imagine what he can do to help.
>
> For example, when I volunteer at community events or donate to charity, I model why it's important to give back and how these actions can positively impact the lives of others. I also use storybooks and role-play to help him understand emotions – whether it's a story of kindness or a tale where someone learns from their mistakes. Through these activities, he is learning not just to observe the world around him, but to engage with it in a thoughtful, compassionate way.
>
> At home, I create a safe space for him to express his feelings. If he's upset, I encourage him to express his emotions. This practice of open communication teaches him to be mindful of his emotions and those of others. By nurturing these traits, I hope he grows into a young man who values kindness, understands the importance of helping others and builds relationships grounded in compassion and empathy.

CHAPTER 4

BUILDING EMOTIONAL INTELLIGENCE IN CHILDREN

'It is very important to understand that emotional intelligence is not the opposite of intelligence, it is not the triumph of heart over head – it is the unique intersection of both.'

– David Caruso, psychologist and EQ expert

In today's rapidly evolving world, emotional intelligence (EQ) is increasingly recognised as a critical factor in life success, often surpassing traditional measures of intelligence (IQ). While IQ is important, especially in academic settings, EQ is what enables individuals to navigate social complexities, build meaningful relationships and manage the emotional challenges life throws at them. For children, developing a strong foundation in emotional intelligence is key to their overall well-being and future success. This chapter will explore the importance of EQ, how to help children identify and express their emotions in healthy ways, teach them to recognise and respect the emotions of others and use emotional regulation as a tool for conflict resolution.

Research by Daniel Goleman (1995), a psychologist and leading expert on emotional intelligence, emphasises that EQ plays a critical role in determining how children manage their emotions and build relationships. Goleman's model of emotional intelligence includes five components: self-awareness, self-regulation, motivation, empathy and social skills. These traits, when developed early in life, help children navigate interpersonal relationships, manage conflict and thrive in social environments. His research shows that children with high emotional intelligence are better equipped to handle stress, exhibit greater resilience in the face of challenges and form more positive, meaningful relationships.

The Importance of EQ Over IQ in Life Success

Emotional intelligence refers to the ability to understand, manage and express emotions effectively, both in oneself and in interactions with others. It includes skills such as self-awareness, empathy, emotional regulation and social competence. Research has shown that individuals with high EQ are better equipped to handle stress, communicate effectively, resolve conflicts and lead successful personal and professional lives.

While IQ might open doors, EQ determines how well someone can navigate through those doors. For example, a child with high IQ may excel in school, but without EQ, they may struggle to form friendships, manage disappointments or work collaboratively with others. Conversely, a child with high EQ can harness their emotional strengths to enhance their academic and social experiences, making them more resilient and adaptable in various life situations.

Teaching children emotional intelligence is not just about helping them succeed academically or socially; it's about equipping them with the tools they need to lead fulfilling, balanced lives. By prioritising EQ, parents can help their children build the emotional resilience necessary to thrive in a complex, interconnected world.

How to Help Children Identify and Express Their Emotions Healthily

One of the first steps in developing emotional intelligence is helping children identify and express their emotions. This process begins with creating an environment where emotions are acknowledged and validated, not dismissed or ignored.

Encourage Emotional Vocabulary

To express emotions, children first need the language to describe them. Parents can help by teaching their children a broad emotional vocabulary. Instead of just using basic words like 'happy', 'sad' or 'angry', encourage them to explore more nuanced emotions, such as 'frustrated', 'disappointed' or 'excited'. When a child can accurately name their emotions, they are better able to express what they are feeling and why.

Model Emotional Expression

Children learn by watching their parents. When parents openly and appropriately express their emotions, they provide a model for their children to follow. For example, if you're feeling overwhelmed, you might say, 'I'm feeling a bit stressed right now, so I'm going to take a few deep breaths to calm down'. This not only shows your child that it's okay to feel stressed but also demonstrates a healthy way to manage that emotion.

Create a Safe Space for Emotions

Children need to feel that their emotions are valid and that it's safe to express them. Encourage your child to talk about their feelings without fear of judgment or punishment. This can be done by setting aside time each day to check in with your child about how they're feeling or by creating a 'feelings jar' where they can write down their emotions and discuss them with you later.

Use Storytelling and Play

Storytelling and play are powerful tools for helping children understand and express their emotions. Reading books that explore different feelings or using role-playing games can make the process of identifying emotions more engaging and less intimidating.

Teaching Children to Recognise and Respect the Emotions of Others

Empathy, a key component of emotional intelligence, involves recognising and respecting the emotions of others. Teaching children to understand and care about how others feel is crucial for building strong, positive relationships.

Practice Active Listening

Active listening is the foundation of empathy. Teach your child to listen to others without interrupting and to pay attention to both what is being said and how it is being said. Encourage them to ask questions that show they are interested in understanding the other person's perspective.

Discuss Emotional Cues

Children need to learn that emotions are not just expressed through words but also through body language, facial expressions and tone of voice. You can help them recognise these cues by discussing how different people look and sound when they are happy, sad, angry or scared. For example, after watching a movie or interacting with others, ask your child how they think the characters or people were feeling and what clues led them to that conclusion.

Encourage Perspective-Taking

Perspective-taking is about putting oneself in another person's shoes. When conflicts arise, ask your child to consider how the other person might be feeling and why. This not only helps them develop empathy but also encourages them to think critically about their own behaviour and its impact on others.

Reinforce Respectful Behaviour

Respecting others' emotions involves more than just understanding them; it requires acting in ways that acknowledge and honour those feelings. Reinforce respectful behaviour by praising your child when they show kindness, consideration or patience towards others, especially in emotionally charged situations.

Emotional Regulation as a Tool for Conflict Resolution

Emotional regulation is the ability to manage and respond to one's emotions in a healthy and constructive manner. It's an essential skill for resolving conflicts, both within oneself and in interactions with others.

Teach Self-Calming Techniques

Children need to learn strategies for calming themselves when they feel overwhelmed by emotions. Techniques such as deep breathing, counting to ten or taking a break can help them regain control and approach situations more calmly. Practise these techniques with your child during moments of calm, so they are ready to use them when emotions run high.

Encourage Problem-Solving

When conflicts arise, guide your child through the process of identifying the problem, considering possible solutions and choosing a course of action. Encourage them to think about how different solutions might make them and others feel, and to choose the one that leads to the most positive outcome. This approach not only helps children resolve conflicts but also reinforces the importance of considering emotions in decision-making.

Model Constructive Conflict Resolution

Children learn how to handle conflicts by watching how their parents handle them. Model constructive conflict resolution by staying calm, expressing your feelings clearly, listening to others and working towards a solution that respects everyone's emotions. Show your child that conflicts don't have to be destructive; they can be opportunities for growth and understanding.

Reinforce the Importance of Apologies

Teaching children to apologise sincerely when they've hurt someone is an important part of emotional regulation. A genuine apology acknowledges the other person's feelings and helps repair the relationship. Encourage your child to express what they are sorry for and how they plan to avoid the same mistake in the future.

Building emotional intelligence in children is one of the most valuable gifts parents can give. By helping children identify and express their emotions, teaching them to recognise and respect the emotions of others, and equipping them with tools for emotional regulation, parents can set their children on a path to successful, fulfilling lives. Emotional intelligence not only contributes to personal happiness and resilience but also plays a crucial role in creating a more compassionate, empathetic and peaceful world.

> When it comes to fostering emotional intelligence in my son who is a toddler, I make it a point to integrate discussions about feelings into our daily routine. I hope to encourage him to express his emotions, whether he's feeling happy, sad, frustrated or excited. For example, if he's upset, I give him a cuddle and sit with him. By validating his emotions, I help him realise that it's okay to feel upset and that the key is learning how to manage those feelings. To further nurture his emotional intelligence, I've introduced calming techniques like going for a walk or taking a break when emotions feel overwhelming. These practices help him regulate his reactions, especially in moments of frustration or anger.
>
> At home, I've created an environment where emotional expression is not only accepted but encouraged. By being open about my own feelings and modelling emotional regulation, I aim to teach him how to balance his emotions while maintaining respect for others. This focus on emotional intelligence has not only strengthened our bond but also helps him develop skills that will benefit him in all areas of his life growing up, academically, socially and personally.

CHAPTER 5

INSTILLING RESPECT FOR SELF AND OTHERS

'Respect yourself and others will respect you.'

– **Confucius, Chinese philosopher**

Respect is a fundamental pillar of healthy, non-violent relationships and a key element in raising children who grow into compassionate, well-adjusted adults. By instilling respect for both oneself and others, parents lay the groundwork for their children to develop a strong sense of self-worth and an understanding of how to interact with others in a positive, non-harmful manner. This chapter will explore the concept of self-respect, the importance of teaching children to respect others' boundaries and differences, how respect fosters healthy relationships and strategies for addressing disrespectful behaviour and bullying.

Research conducted by Dr. Thomas Lickona (1991), a developmental psychologist and expert on character education, emphasises that teaching children respect is crucial for their moral development. Lickona argues that respect for oneself and others is foundational for ethical behaviour and healthy relationships. His work suggests that children learn respect not only through direct instruction but also by observing respectful behaviour modelled by their caregivers. Furthermore, children who are taught to respect others' boundaries and differences are more likely to develop empathy, exhibit prosocial behaviour and avoid conflict. These qualities lead to stronger, more harmonious relationships both in childhood and later in life.

The Concept of Self-Respect and Its Importance in Developing Self-Worth

Self-respect is the foundation of a person's self-worth. It involves recognising one's own value, setting healthy boundaries and treating oneself with kindness and dignity. When children are taught to respect themselves, they develop a sense of worth that is not dependent on external validation but comes from within. This internal sense of value is crucial for building confidence and resilience, which are essential for navigating life's challenges.

Model Self-Respect

Children learn about self-respect by observing how their parents treat themselves. If you demonstrate self-respect by setting boundaries, prioritising self-care and speaking kindly about yourself, your child is more likely to adopt these behaviours. For example, if you make time for your own hobbies and interests, it shows your child that it's important to value one's own needs and passions.

Encourage Positive Self-Talk

Teach your child to speak kindly to themselves, especially in moments of frustration or failure. Instead of harsh self-criticism, encourage them to use constructive language. For example, instead of saying, 'I'm so bad at this', they might say, 'I'm still learning, and I'll get better with practise'. This kind of positive self-talk reinforces their sense of self-worth and helps them approach challenges with a growth mindset.

Teach Boundary-Setting

Part of self-respect is knowing how to set and maintain boundaries. Help your child understand that it's okay to say no to things that make them uncomfortable or that go against their values. Role-playing different scenarios can be a helpful way to practise boundary-setting. For example, you could pretend to be a peer-pressuring them to do something they don't want to do and then guide them through how to respond assertively.

Teaching Respect for Others' Boundaries and Differences

Respecting others is just as important as respecting oneself. It involves recognising and honouring the boundaries, feelings and differences of others. When children learn to respect others, they develop empathy and build stronger, more harmonious relationships.

Discuss the Concept of Boundaries

Explain to your child that everyone has boundaries and limits that define what they are comfortable with and what they are not. Teach them that respecting these boundaries is crucial in maintaining healthy relationships. Use examples from everyday life to illustrate this concept. For instance, if a friend doesn't want to share a toy, it's important to respect that decision.

Celebrate Diversity

Help your child understand and appreciate the differences in people's backgrounds, cultures and perspectives. Encourage them to be curious and open-minded, rather than judgmental. You can do this by exposing them to diverse cultures through books, movies and experiences, and by discussing the importance of valuing people for who they are.

Reinforce the Golden Rule

The principle of treating others as you would like to be treated is a simple yet powerful way to teach respect. Encourage your child to think about how their actions and words affect others and to strive to act in ways that are kind, considerate and respectful.

How Respect Fosters Healthy, Non-Violent Relationships

Respect is the cornerstone of healthy relationships. It fosters trust, understanding and mutual regard, creating a strong foundation for non-violent interactions.

Building Trust

Trust is built when people feel respected and valued. Teach your child that trust is earned through consistent actions that show care and consideration for others' feelings and boundaries. When children learn to respect others, they are more likely to develop trusting, supportive relationships.

Promoting Healthy Communication

Respectful communication involves listening actively, speaking kindly and being open to others' perspectives. Encourage your child to practise these skills in their interactions with friends, family and peers. This not only helps prevent misunderstandings and conflicts but also strengthens their ability to resolve disagreements peacefully.

Preventing Violence

Violence often stems from a lack of respect, whether it's disrespect for oneself, others or differences between people. By teaching children to value respect, you reduce the likelihood of them engaging in or tolerating violent behaviour. When respect is the norm, there is less room for aggression, bullying or abusive behaviour in relationships.

Addressing Disrespectful Behaviour and Bullying

Despite best efforts, children may sometimes exhibit disrespectful behaviour or encounter bullying, either as perpetrators or victims. Addressing these behaviours promptly and effectively is crucial in maintaining a culture of respect.

Address Disrespect Immediately

When your child displays disrespectful behaviour, address it calmly but firmly. Explain why the behaviour is unacceptable and discuss how it made the other person feel. For example, if your child interrupts someone while they're speaking, you might say, 'It's important to let others finish speaking before you respond. How do you think they felt when you interrupted them?'

Encourage Accountability

Teach your child to take responsibility for their actions. If they've disrespected someone, encourage them to apologise sincerely and to think about how they can make amends. This not only helps repair the relationship but also reinforces the importance of owning up to one's mistakes.

Empower Your Child to Stand Up Against Bullying

If your child witnesses or experiences bullying, empower them to speak up. Teach them strategies for standing up to bullies in a safe and effective manner and encourage them to seek help from a trusted adult if needed. Reinforce that bullying is never acceptable and that everyone has the right to be treated with respect.

Provide Support and Guidance

Children who engage in disrespectful behaviour or bullying may be struggling with underlying issues, such as low self-esteem or peer pressure. Provide them with the support and guidance they need to address these issues and to develop healthier ways of interacting with others.

Instilling respect for oneself and others is essential in raising children who can build strong, non-violent relationships. By teaching your child the importance of self-respect, encouraging them to honour others' boundaries and differences, and addressing disrespectful behaviour and bullying, you are helping them develop the skills they need to navigate the complexities of human relationships with kindness, empathy and integrity. Respect not only creates a foundation for healthy interactions but also plays a vital role in building a more peaceful and compassionate world.

> Raising my two-year-old son with a focus on respect starts with small, everyday moments. At this age, he's learning to assert his independence, which makes it the perfect time to teach him about boundaries and how to treat others with kindness. For example, when he plays with our family dog, I guide him to be gentle and explain that just as he likes his personal space, our dog does too. By encouraging him to be mindful of the dog's feelings, I am already laying the foundation for understanding boundaries and respect for others.
>
> I also teach him about self-respect through positive reinforcement. Whenever he accomplishes something, whether it's picking up his toys or trying something new, I celebrate his efforts and let him know that he should be proud of himself. This helps him develop a sense of self-worth, which is essential as he grows.
>
> To model respect in our household, I make sure to listen to him attentively, even when he's expressing himself in ways that are typical for a toddler, like frustration or excitement. By showing him that his feelings matter, I'm teaching him to respect his own emotions and, in turn, the emotions of others. Though he's still young, these early lessons are crucial for helping him understand the importance of both self-respect and respect for those around him.

CHAPTER 6

ENCOURAGING RESPONSIBILITY AND ACCOUNTABILITY

'The price of greatness is responsibility.'

– Winston Churchill, former British prime minister

Responsibility and accountability are vital components in developing well-rounded individuals who contribute positively to their families and communities. When children learn to take responsibility for their actions and understand the importance of accountability, they build trust, integrity and the capacity for collaboration. This chapter explores the role of responsibility in personal and family life, strategies for teaching children to take responsibility for their actions, the significance of accountability and how fostering responsibility can prevent the blame game and encourage teamwork.

In their research on child development, Dr. Robert Brooks and Dr. Sam Goldstein (2001), co-authors of *Raising Resilient Children*, emphasise the importance of responsibility in fostering resilience and self-discipline in children. They argue that when children are given age-appropriate responsibilities, they learn problem-solving skills, develop a sense of competence and strengthen their ability to handle future challenges. Their work shows that teaching responsibility should be gradual, beginning with small tasks, and expanding as the child grows older. Accountability, on the other hand, helps children understand the consequences of

The Role of Responsibility in Personal and Family Life

A functional and harmonious family life relies on responsibility of a functional and harmonious family life. It involves recognising one's duties and obligations within the family and understanding the impact of one's actions on others. Teaching children about responsibility helps them develop a sense of ownership over their behaviour and decisions, which is crucial for their growth into conscientious adults.

Cultivating a Sense of Duty

In a family setting, every member has roles and duties that contribute to the household's smooth operation. Whether it's helping with chores, taking care of pets or completing homework, these responsibilities teach children that their actions matter and have consequences. By assigning age-appropriate tasks, you help your child understand that being part of a family means contributing to its well-being.

Building Self-Esteem Through Responsibility

When children successfully fulfil their responsibilities, it boosts their self-esteem and confidence. They begin to see themselves as capable and reliable individuals, which is a significant factor in developing a strong sense of self-worth. Praise and encouragement when they complete their tasks reinforce this positive self-image.

Promoting Independence

Responsibility also fosters independence. As children learn to manage their tasks and obligations, they gain the skills necessary to function autonomously. This independence is essential as they grow older and face more complex challenges, both within and outside the family environment.

Teaching Children to Take Responsibility for Their Actions

One of the most important aspects of responsibility is taking ownership of one's actions. Children need to understand that their choices have consequences and that they are accountable for those consequences, whether positive or negative.

Lead by Example

Demonstrate responsible behaviour in your actions and decisions and your child is likely to mimic this. For example, if you make a mistake, admit it openly and discuss how you plan to rectify it. This shows your child that taking responsibility is a normal and healthy part of life.

Encourage Decision-Making

Give your child opportunities to make decisions, even if they are small ones. Whether it's choosing what to wear or deciding how to spend their allowance, decision-making teaches children to weigh options and consider the potential outcomes of their choices. This practice helps them understand the link between actions and consequences.

Discuss Consequences

When your child makes a mistake or behaves inappropriately, use it as a teaching moment. Instead of simply punishing them, have a conversation about what happened, why it was wrong and what they can do differently next time. This approach encourages them to think critically about their actions and to learn from their mistakes.

Reinforce Accountability

Hold your child accountable for their actions by setting clear expectations and consistent consequences. If they fail to complete a task or behave irresponsibly, follow through with the agreed-upon consequence. Consistency helps children understand that they are responsible for their choices and that their actions have real-world implications.

The Importance of Accountability in Building Trust and Integrity

Accountability is closely tied to trust and integrity. When children learn to be accountable, they become more trustworthy and reliable, qualities that are essential in all relationships.

Building Trust Through Accountability

Trust is built when people know they can count on each other to follow through on commitments. Teach your child that being accountable means doing what they say they will do. This could be as simple as completing their homework on time or keeping a promise to a friend. Over time, these small acts of accountability build a reputation of trustworthiness.

Developing Integrity

Integrity involves being honest and having strong moral principles. Accountability is a key component of integrity because it requires a person to be honest about their actions and to take responsibility when they fall short. Encourage your child to be honest about their mistakes and to take corrective action, which helps them develop a strong sense of integrity.

Encouraging Open Communication

Accountability also involves open communication. Teach your child to communicate openly about their responsibilities and any challenges they may face in fulfilling them. This openness fosters a culture of transparency and mutual support within the family, where everyone feels comfortable discussing their responsibilities and seeking help when needed.

How Responsibility Helps Prevent the Blame Game and Fosters Collaboration

In many situations, when things go wrong, people tend to shift the blame onto others. This 'blame game' can create tension and conflict within families. Teaching children to take responsibility helps prevent this behaviour and encourages a collaborative approach to problem-solving.

Addressing the Blame Game

When a problem arises, it's easy to point fingers and avoid responsibility. However, this approach only creates more conflict and prevents effective resolution. Teach your child that it's more important to focus on solving the problem than on assigning blame. Encourage them to ask, 'What can we do to fix this?' instead of, 'Whose fault is this?'

Promoting Teamwork

Responsibility and accountability promote a sense of teamwork. When everyone in the family takes responsibility for their actions and works together to solve problems, it creates a more supportive and harmonious environment. Encourage collaborative problem-solving by involving your child in discussions about how to address family issues or challenges. This not only teaches them responsibility but also fosters a sense of belonging and cooperation.

Celebrating Collaborative Successes

When your family successfully works together to overcome a challenge, take time to celebrate the achievement. This reinforces the idea that collaboration, responsibility and accountability lead to positive outcomes. It also encourages your child to continue practicing these values in future situations.

Encouraging responsibility and accountability in children is crucial for their development into responsible, trustworthy and collaborative adults. By teaching them the importance of responsibility in personal and family life, helping them take ownership of their actions and fostering accountability, you equip them with the tools they need to build trust, integrity and strong relationships. Moreover, by preventing the blame game and promoting a culture of collaboration, you create a family environment where everyone feels valued, supported and empowered to contribute to the greater good.

> With my two-year-old son, I gently introduce accountability by guiding him to reflect on his behaviour, especially when he makes a mistake, like spilling juice or being rough during play. Instead of reacting with frustration, I calmly explain the impact of his actions and ask him to help clean up or make things right. By framing these moments as learning opportunities, I'm teaching him that mistakes happen, but that it's important to take responsibility and fix them. This approach not only builds his confidence but also strengthens his ability to take accountability for his actions as he grows.
>
> It's rewarding to watch him take on these small responsibilities with pride, knowing that these early lessons will shape his sense of integrity and his willingness to contribute positively to his surroundings.

CHAPTER 7

FOSTERING POSITIVE TRAITS IN BOYS

'We've begun to raise daughters more like sons ... but few have the courage to raise our sons more like our daughters.'

– Gloria Steinem, feminist, journalist and social political activist

In a world where traditional views of masculinity often equate strength with stoicism and dominance, it is essential to redefine what it means to be a man. Positive traits like vulnerability, empathy and kindness are crucial in breaking down harmful stereotypes that have long been associated with male identity. By fostering positive traits, we can raise boys who grow into men that respect and uplift others, ultimately contributing to a more compassionate and equitable society. This chapter explores the redefinition of masculinity, the importance of breaking harmful stereotypes, the role of male role models and how to raise boys to embody positive masculinity.

According to Dr. Michael Kimmel (2008), one of the world's leading experts on men and masculinities, traditional masculinity is often defined by harmful cultural norms that promote aggression, emotional repression and dominance. In his book *Guyland: The Perilous World Where Boys Become Men*, Kimmel argues that these outdated views of masculinity contribute to a 'boy crisis', where young men struggle to navigate societal expectations while suppressing traits like vulnerability and compassion. He advocates for redefining masculinity by teaching boys emotional intelligence and encouraging positive traits like empathy and kindness, which not only benefits the boys themselves but also improves the communities and relationships they are part of.

Redefining Masculinity to Include Vulnerability, Empathy and Kindness

Traditionally, masculinity has been defined by traits such as toughness, emotional restraint and self-reliance. While these characteristics can be valuable in certain contexts, they often come at the cost of emotional well-being and healthy relationships. Positive traits, on the other hand, encourage men and boys to embrace a broader range of human experiences and emotions, including vulnerability, empathy and kindness.

Embracing Vulnerability

Vulnerability is often seen as a weakness in traditional masculine norms. However, it is, in fact, a source of strength. When boys and men are encouraged to express their feelings, admit their fears and seek help when needed, they become more resilient and capable of forming deep, meaningful connections with others. Teaching boys that it's okay to cry, ask for support or show emotion is crucial in helping them develop into emotionally healthy adults.

Cultivating Empathy

Empathy is the ability to understand and share the feelings of others. When boys learn to be empathetic, they become more attuned to the needs and emotions of those around them. This not only makes them better friends, partners and community members but also helps them navigate their own emotions more effectively. Empathy fosters kindness, reduces aggression and promotes peaceful conflict resolution, which are all essential qualities for a healthy and balanced life.

Encouraging Kindness

Kindness is a powerful expression of positive traits. When boys are taught to be kind, they learn to treat others with respect and compassion, regardless of gender, race or background. Kindness challenges the notion that masculinity is about power over others and instead frames it as the power to uplift and support others. By promoting kindness as a valued trait, we help boys grow into men who contribute positively to society.

Breaking Down Harmful Stereotypes Associated with Traditional Masculinity

The traditional view of masculinity is often associated with a narrow set of behaviours and attitudes, such as dominance, emotional suppression and aggression. These stereotypes can be harmful, leading to a range of negative outcomes, including mental health issues, violence and strained relationships. To foster positive masculinity, it is essential to break down these harmful stereotypes and replace them with healthier, more inclusive models of manhood.

Challenging the 'Tough Guy' Image

The idea that men must always be tough and stoic is a pervasive stereotype that can prevent boys from expressing their true selves. This image often leads to the suppression of emotions, resulting in unresolved feelings that can manifest as anger, depression or anxiety. By challenging this stereotype and encouraging boys to be open about their emotions, we can help them develop a more balanced and healthy approach to life.

Redefining Strength

Strength is often equated with physical power and emotional detachment in traditional masculinity. However, true strength lies in the ability to face challenges with courage, to be vulnerable and to show compassion towards others. Redefining strength in this way allows boys to understand that being strong doesn't mean being unfeeling or aggressive; it means being resilient, empathetic and kind in the face of adversity.

Addressing Aggression

Aggression is another stereotype often linked to masculinity, where boys are expected to be competitive, assertive and sometimes even confrontational. While assertiveness can be a positive trait when used appropriately, unchecked aggression can lead to harmful behaviours, including violence. By teaching boys to channel their energy into constructive outlets and to resolve conflicts peacefully, we can help them avoid the pitfalls of aggressive behaviour.

The Importance of Male Role Models Who Embody Positive Traits

Role models play a crucial role in shaping a child's understanding of what it means to be a man. Boys look up to the men in their lives – whether it's a father, teacher, coach or public figure – and often model their behaviour after them. It is therefore essential that boys have male role models who embody the principles of positive masculinity.

Leading by Example

Male role models who demonstrate vulnerability, empathy and kindness in their daily lives provide a powerful example for boys to follow. When a father openly expresses his emotions, or a coach emphasises teamwork and respect over winning at all costs, they show boys that positive masculinity is not only acceptable but admirable. These role models help boys understand that being a good man involves more than just physical strength or stoicism; it involves being a caring and responsible individual.

Providing Guidance

Role models also provide guidance on how to navigate the challenges of growing up. Boys often face societal pressures to conform to traditional masculine norms and having a positive role model can help them resist these pressures. A role model who values honesty, respect and emotional intelligence can offer practical advice and support, helping boys to stay true to themselves and their values.

Challenging Negative Influences

In a world where media and peer influences often promote harmful stereotypes of masculinity, positive male role models are more important than ever. These role models can counteract the negative messages boys receive by offering an alternative vision of what it means to be a man – one that is inclusive, respectful and compassionate. By actively engaging with boys and discussing these issues, role models can help them develop a healthy and balanced understanding of masculinity.

Raising Boys to Become Men Who Respect and Uplift Others

The ultimate goal of fostering positive masculinity is to raise boys who grow into men who respect and uplift others. This involves teaching boys to value themselves and those around them, to embrace diversity and to act with integrity in all aspects of their lives.

Teaching Respect

Respect is a fundamental aspect of positive masculinity. Boys need to learn to respect themselves, their peers and those in positions of authority. This respect extends to understanding and appreciating differences, whether they be cultural, gender-based or ideological. By teaching boys to respect others, we help them build healthy, non-violent relationships based on mutual understanding and trust.

Encouraging Uplifting Behaviour

Positive masculinity is about uplifting others, not putting them down. Encourage boys to support their friends, celebrate others' successes and stand up against bullying and injustice. This behaviour not only fosters a sense of community but also reinforces the idea that true masculinity is about lifting others up rather than asserting dominance over them.

Building Integrity

Integrity involves being honest, fair and consistent in one's actions. It's a key component of positive masculinity, as it ensures that boys grow into men who are reliable, trustworthy and principled. Teaching boys the importance of integrity in both their personal and professional lives helps them build a reputation of respect and honour, which in turn allows them to positively influence those around them.

Fostering positive masculinity is a critical step in raising boys who will grow into men that contribute to a more just and compassionate world. By redefining masculinity to include vulnerability, empathy and kindness, breaking down harmful stereotypes, emphasising the importance of male role models and raising boys to respect and uplift others, we can help create a future where men are not only strong but also emotionally intelligent, compassionate and respectful. These qualities are not only vital for the individual's success and well-being but also for building stronger, healthier and more resilient families and communities.

Raising my son, I actively focus on nurturing traits like empathy, kindness and emotional expression, even at his young age. One way I encourage this is by helping him identify and express his emotions. If he's upset, instead of saying, 'You're okay', I ask him, 'Are you feeling sad or frustrated?' This helps him understand that it's okay to have emotions, and it's even more important to express them in a healthy way. I believe that by validating his feelings, I'm teaching him that vulnerability is a strength, not a weakness.

Another way I foster empathy is through modelling kindness and inclusion in everyday interactions. Whether we're playing with other children at the park or interacting with family members, I make it a point to show kindness and explain the importance of being thoughtful towards others. For example, if he sees someone else feeling sad, I encourage him to offer a hug or share his toys. In moments like these, I remind him that caring for others is an important part of being a good person.

By instilling these values early, I hope to raise him with a mindset that challenges the traditional stereotypes of masculinity, and instead helps him grow into a man who is compassionate, empathetic and confident in expressing his emotions. My goal is for him to learn that strength doesn't come from dominance but from kindness, respect and emotional intelligence.

CHAPTER 8

EMPOWERING GIRLS TO STAND UP FOR THEMSELVES'

'I raise up my voice – not so I can shout but so that those without a voice can be heard ... We cannot all succeed when half of us are held back.'

– Malala Yousafzai, Pakistani activist for female education and the youngest Nobel Prize laureate

Empowering girls to stand up for themselves is a crucial step towards creating a society where everyone is treated with respect and dignity. In a world where gender inequality still exists, teaching girls to recognise their worth, assert their boundaries and cultivate self-confidence is essential for their personal growth and safety. This chapter explores the importance of empowering girls, addressing societal pressures and the role empowered women play in breaking the cycle of family violence.

Research by Dr. Lisa Hinkelman (2013), author of *Girls Without Limits: Helping Girls Succeed in Relationships, Academics, Careers and Life*, highlights that empowering young girls is critical in navigating societal pressures and achieving self-actualisation. Hinkelman emphasises that instilling self-confidence and assertiveness in girls helps them develop the skills needed to stand up for themselves in difficult situations, whether in school, personal relationships or future workplaces. Furthermore, teaching girls to assert their boundaries and make empowered decisions about their bodies is a critical component in preventing gender-based violence and breaking the cycle of family abuse.

Teaching Girls to Recognise Their Worth and Assert Their Boundaries

From a young age, it is vital to teach girls that they have inherent value and deserve to be treated with respect. Recognising their worth is the foundation of self-esteem and the key to establishing healthy relationships. When girls understand their value, they are better equipped to assert their boundaries and resist any form of mistreatment or abuse.

Building Self-Worth

Self-worth is the understanding that one deserves love, respect and opportunities simply by being who they are. Girls must be encouraged to appreciate their unique qualities and capabilities, whether it's their intelligence, creativity or compassion. Parents, educators and mentors play a critical role in affirming these traits and fostering a positive self-image. Praise should be focused not only on achievements but also on the effort, resilience and kindness that girls display. When girls feel valued, they are more likely to set high standards for how they should be treated by others.

Asserting Boundaries

Teaching girls to assert their boundaries is essential for their safety and well-being. Boundaries are the limits they set to protect their physical, emotional and mental health. Girls should be taught that it's okay to say no and that their comfort and consent are non-negotiable. Whether it's in friendships, relationships or even interactions with authority figures, girls need to know that they have the right to stand up for themselves and protect their personal space. Practising scenarios where they might need to assert boundaries can give them the confidence to do so in real situations.

Encouraging Self-Confidence and Independence in Girls

Self-confidence and independence are two of the most empowering qualities a girl can possess. They enable girls to pursue their goals, make decisions and navigate life's challenges with resilience and determination. Fostering these traits from an early age sets the stage for a lifetime of empowerment.

Nurturing Self-Confidence

Self-confidence arises from a belief in one's abilities and the courage to take risks and face challenges. Girls should be encouraged to try new things, even if they seem difficult or unfamiliar. Successes, big or small, should be celebrated, and failures should be seen as opportunities for growth rather than setbacks. Encouraging girls to voice their opinions, share their ideas and participate in decision-making processes helps them build confidence in their judgment and capabilities. This confidence becomes a powerful tool as they grow, enabling them to challenge gender norms and assert their rights.

Promoting Independence

Independence is about giving girls the freedom to explore, learn and make decisions for themselves. While guidance is essential, allowing girls to take responsibility for their actions and make choices fosters a sense of autonomy. This can be as simple as letting them choose their clothes, manage their time or pursue hobbies they are passionate about. As they grow older, encouraging them to set personal goals, whether academic, athletic or creative, teaches them to rely on themselves and their abilities. Independence empowers girls to lead their own lives, free from the constraints of societal expectations.

Addressing Societal Pressures and Stereotypes That Undermine Girls' Empowerment

Despite significant progress in gender equality, societal pressures and stereotypes still exist that undermine girls' empowerment. These pressures often dictate how girls should look, behave and what roles they should aspire to, limiting their potential and self-expression.

Challenging Beauty Standards

One of the most pervasive pressures girls face is the societal obsession with beauty standards. From a young age, girls are bombarded with images and messages that equate their worth with their appearance. It is crucial to counteract these messages by teaching girls that their value lies far beyond their looks. Encouraging them to focus on their talents, skills and character rather than their physical appearance helps them build self-esteem based on substance, not superficiality. Girls should be reminded that beauty is diverse and that being true to themselves is far more important than conforming to narrow ideals.

Breaking Gender Stereotypes

Gender stereotypes often limit girls' opportunities and aspirations. Stereotypes suggest that girls should be passive, nurturing and confined to certain roles, while boys are encouraged to be assertive and pursue careers in science, technology and leadership. It's essential to challenge these stereotypes by providing girls with diverse role models and encouraging them to explore all fields, from science and sports to leadership and the arts. Girls should be taught that they can be anything they want to be and their gender does not dictate their capabilities or potential.

Addressing the Media's Role

The media plays a significant role in shaping societal norms and expectations. Unfortunately, media portrayals of women often reinforce stereotypes, depicting them as either overly sexualised or in subordinate roles. It's important to educate girls about media literacy, helping them to critically analyse the content they consume and recognise when it perpetuates harmful stereotypes. Encouraging them to seek out and support media that showcases strong, diverse female characters can help counteract these negative influences.

How Empowered Women Contribute to Breaking the Cycle of Family Violence

Empowered women are a formidable force in breaking the cycle of family violence. When girls grow into women who are confident, independent and assertive, they are less likely to become victims of abuse and more likely to advocate for themselves and others. Empowered women contribute to the dismantling of patriarchal structures that perpetuate violence and inequality.

Standing Up Against Abuse

Women who have been empowered from a young age are more likely to recognise abusive behaviour and take action to protect themselves. They are equipped with the self-esteem, knowledge and support systems necessary to leave abusive relationships and seek help. Empowered women are also more likely to speak out against family violence, raising awareness and advocating for change in their communities.

Breaking the Silence

One of the most significant barriers to addressing family violence is the culture of silence that surrounds it. Empowered women are often at the forefront of breaking this silence, sharing their stories and encouraging others to do the same. By speaking out, they challenge the stigma associated with family violence and help create a culture where abuse is not tolerated. Their voices are vital in pushing for legal and social reforms that protect victims and hold abusers accountable.

Role Models for the Next Generation

Empowered women serve as role models for the next generation of girls. When young girls see women who are strong, independent and vocal about their rights, they are inspired to follow in their footsteps. These role models demonstrate that it is possible to overcome adversity, achieve success and live a life free from violence. By passing on the lessons of empowerment, they help ensure that future generations of girls are even better equipped to stand up for themselves and continue the fight against family violence.

Empowering girls to stand up for themselves is not just about protecting them from harm; it's about giving them the tools to lead fulfilling, independent lives and to challenge the structures that perpetuate inequality and violence. By teaching girls to recognise their worth, assert their boundaries, build self-confidence and challenge societal pressures, we can help them grow into empowered women who contribute to breaking the cycle of family violence. These empowered women will not only shape their own destinies but also create a ripple effect that influences entire communities, paving the way for a more just and equitable world.

Raising my son, I place a strong emphasis on understanding boundaries, particularly when interacting with others, including girls. Even at the young age of two, it's important to introduce the concept of consent in simple terms. For example, when playing with other children, I always remind him to ask, 'Is it okay if I give you a hug?' or, 'Can I play with your toy?' This teaches him from an early age that everyone's personal space and feelings should be respected, and consent must be obtained before any form of physical contact.

When we interact with family members or friends, I never force him to hug or kiss anyone if he doesn't feel comfortable. I explain to him that it's okay to say no and that his body belongs to him. By teaching him these concepts now, I hope to raise a son who understands that consent is essential in every interaction, helping to foster respect and equality as he grows older.

Moreover, I also model assertiveness and mutual respect in my own interactions, ensuring that he sees how important it is to ask for and respect the boundaries of others, regardless of gender. My goal is to raise a boy who not only respects girls but values them as equals, laying the foundation for healthy, respectful relationships in the future.

CHAPTER 9

PROMOTING HEALTHY COMMUNICATION SKILLS

'The single biggest problem in communication is the illusion that it has taken place.'

– George Bernard Shaw, Irish playwright and critic

Effective communication is crucial in preventing and resolving conflicts. By teaching children how to express themselves clearly, listen actively and interpret non-verbal cues, parents can foster open and respectful dialogues within the family. This chapter explores the importance of communication skills, provides practical strategies for teaching these skills and offers guidance on addressing and overcoming communication breakdowns.

Research conducted by 'Dr. John Gottman' (1997), a psychologist known for his work on marital stability and communication, emphasises that teaching children healthy communication skills early in life is a crucial determinant of their future success in relationships. Gottman's studies show that children who learn to express their emotions and thoughts openly and who are taught to listen and validate others' feelings tend to have more resilient and empathetic relationships as adults. These skills help prevent misunderstandings, reduce conflicts and foster emotional intimacy, contributing to healthier dynamics in all areas of life. By incorporating practices like active listening, emotional validation and conflict resolution, parents can significantly reduce communication breakdowns in family settings.

The Role of Effective Communication in Preventing and Resolving Conflicts

Effective communication plays a pivotal role in both preventing and resolving conflicts. When family members can express their thoughts, feelings and concerns openly and respectfully, misunderstandings are minimised, and conflicts are more easily resolved.

Preventing Conflicts

Clear and honest communication helps prevent conflicts by ensuring that everyone's needs and expectations are understood. When family members communicate effectively, they are less likely to misinterpret each other's intentions or make assumptions that could lead to disagreements. Encouraging open discussions about feelings, needs and expectations helps create a proactive approach to conflict prevention.

Resolving Conflicts

In the event of a conflict, effective communication is essential for resolution. It allows family members to discuss their perspectives, understand each other's viewpoints and work together to find mutually acceptable solutions. Communication skills such as active listening, empathy and assertiveness are key to resolving conflicts in a constructive and non-confrontational manner.

Teaching Active Listening, Clear Expression and Non-Verbal Cues

Teaching children how to communicate effectively involves several key components: active listening, clear expression and understanding non-verbal cues.

Active Listening

Active listening is the practice of fully focusing on and understanding what another person is saying. It involves giving the speaker your full attention, acknowledging their feelings and responding thoughtfully. To teach active listening:

- ◊ Model the behaviour: Demonstrate active listening in your interactions. Show that you are engaged by making eye contact, nodding and giving verbal acknowledgments like 'I see' or 'I understand'.

- ◊ Practise listening skills: Engage in activities that encourage listening, such as storytelling or role-playing exercises. Ask your child to listen to a story and then summarise it to ensure they've understood the main points.

- ◊ Teach reflection: Encourage your child to reflect back what they've heard by using phrases like, 'So what you're saying is …' This helps ensure they've correctly interpreted the message and shows that they value the speaker's perspective.

Clear Expression

Clear expression involves articulating thoughts and feelings in a way that is understandable and respectful. To promote clear expression:

- ◊ Encourage use of 'I' statements: Teach your child to use 'I' statements to express their feelings and needs without blaming others. For example, 'I feel upset when you interrupt me because I need to finish my thoughts' is more constructive than, 'You always interrupt me'.

- ◊ Practise articulation: Help your child practise expressing their thoughts and feelings clearly through conversation games or writing exercises. Encourage them to think about what they want to say and how to say it effectively.

Non-Verbal Cues

Non-verbal communication, such as body language, facial expressions and tone of voice, conveys important information and can impact the message being communicated. To teach non-verbal communication:

- ◊ Discuss body language: Explain how body language, such as crossed arms or avoiding eye contact, can affect communication. Teach your child to be aware of their own body language and to interpret others' non-verbal cues.

- ◊ Role-play situations: Use role-playing to practise different non-verbal cues and their meanings. This helps children understand how body language can influence conversations and relationships.

How to Foster Open Dialogue Within the Family

Creating an environment where open dialogue is encouraged helps build trust and understanding within the family. Open dialogue allows family members to share their thoughts and feelings without fear of judgment or retaliation.

Create a Safe Space

Establish a safe and supportive environment where family members feel comfortable expressing themselves. This includes being non-judgmental, actively listening and validating each other's experiences and emotions. Let your child know that their thoughts and feelings are valued and encourage them to speak openly.

Schedule Regular Check-Ins

Set aside regular times for family discussions, where everyone can share their thoughts and feelings. This could be during family meals, weekly meetings or designated family time. Regular check-ins help maintain open lines of communication and address any issues before they escalate.

Encourage Open Questions

Encourage family members to ask open-ended questions that invite discussion and exploration. For example, instead of asking, 'Did you have a good day?' ask, 'What was the best part of your day?' Open-ended questions promote deeper conversations and help family members connect on a more meaningful level.

Addressing Communication Breakdowns and Restoring Understanding

Despite best efforts, communication breakdowns can occur. Addressing these breakdowns promptly and effectively is essential to restoring understanding and maintaining healthy relationships.

Identify the Issue

When a communication breakdown happens, identify the root cause of the issue. This may involve misunderstandings, misinterpretations or emotional reactions. Discuss the problem openly and honestly to understand each other's perspectives.

Apologise and Forgive

If the breakdown involved hurtful behaviour or statements, offer a sincere apology and seek forgiveness. Acknowledge any mistakes or misunderstandings and express a commitment to improving communication in the future. Forgiveness helps heal wounds and rebuild trust.

Develop Solutions Together

Work together to develop solutions to prevent future communication breakdowns. This may involve setting guidelines for respectful communication, practising active listening or improving non-verbal cues. By addressing the issue collaboratively, family members can strengthen their communication skills and enhance their relationships.

Seek Professional Help If Needed

If communication breakdowns persist or become more serious, consider seeking professional help, such as family counselling or therapy. A trained therapist can provide guidance and strategies for improving communication and resolving underlying issues.

Promoting healthy communication skills is vital for fostering strong, respectful relationships and preventing conflicts within the family. By teaching active listening, clear expression and understanding non-verbal cues, parents can help their children develop effective communication skills that will serve them well throughout their lives. Fostering open dialogue, addressing communication breakdowns and seeking professional help when needed are essential for maintaining healthy family dynamics and building resilience.

> With my two-year-old son, I make communication a daily practice by encouraging him to articulate his feelings, even if they are still in simple terms. For instance, when he's upset or frustrated, instead of immediately resolving the issue for him, I gently ask, 'Can you tell me why you're feeling sad or mad?' This helps him connect with his emotions and develop the vocabulary to express himself.
>
> One way I promote healthy communication is through modelling. At home, I make a point of narrating my own feelings in ways he can understand, like saying, 'Mummy feels happy because you cleaned up your toys', or, 'Mummy feels frustrated because we're running late, but we can fix it by hurrying'. This transparency not only teaches him that it's okay to express emotions, but also that communication can be a way to resolve challenges constructively.

I also focus on teaching him active listening by getting down to his eye level when he speaks and repeating his words back to him, which makes him feel heard and valued. This simple but powerful technique helps him see the importance of listening to others, even at such a young age.

As he grows, my goal is to continue fostering open communication, encouraging him to share his thoughts and feelings while teaching him the importance of listening to others. These foundational skills will equip him to build strong, respectful relationships throughout his life.

CHAPTER 10

TEACHING CONFLICT RESOLUTION AND PROBLEM-SOLVING SKILLS

'Conflict is inevitable, but combat is optional.'

– Max Lucado, American author and pastor

Conflict is a natural part of family life, but how we handle disagreements can significantly impact our relationships and overall family dynamics. Teaching children effective conflict resolution and problem-solving skills is crucial for maintaining peace and harmony within the home. This chapter explores the importance of peaceful conflict resolution, offers practical strategies for teaching these skills and provides guidance on how to model conflict resolution as a parent.

Conflict resolution is a critical life skill that significantly affects interpersonal relationships and emotional well-being. According to a study published in the *Journal of Family Psychology* (2007), children who learn effective conflict resolution skills are more likely to develop healthy relationships and exhibit prosocial behaviour. The research indicates that parents who model positive conflict resolution strategies help their children understand how to manage disagreements constructively, leading to improved communication and emotional regulation. Teaching children to approach conflicts with empathy and understanding creates a harmonious home environment and equips them with the tools to handle challenges in their future relationships and communities.

The Importance of Peaceful Conflict Resolution in Family Life

Peaceful conflict resolution is essential for creating a harmonious family environment and fostering healthy relationships. When conflicts are resolved constructively, it helps build trust, respect and understanding among family members.

This approach also sets a positive example for children, teaching them how to handle disagreements in a non-violent and respectful manner.

Reducing Stress and Tension

Peaceful conflict resolution helps reduce stress and tension within the family. When conflicts are handled calmly and respectfully, it prevents escalation and creates a more supportive and loving environment.

This, in turn, promotes emotional well-being and stability for all family members.

Strengthening Relationships

Addressing conflicts constructively strengthens relationships by allowing family members to express their feelings and needs openly. It also provides opportunities for empathy, compromise and mutual understanding, which helps build stronger bonds and resolve issues effectively.

Teaching Life Skills

Learning how to resolve conflicts peacefully and solve problems effectively are valuable life skills that children will carry with them into adulthood. These skills contribute to their personal growth and success in various aspects of life, including school, work and social relationships.

Practical Strategies for Teaching Children to Resolve Conflicts Without Resorting to Violence

Teaching children how to resolve conflicts peacefully involves providing them with practical strategies and tools they can use in challenging situations. Here are some effective approaches:

Encourage Open Communication

Guide children in expressing their feelings and concerns in a direct and honest way. Encourage them to use 'I' statements to articulate their emotions and needs without accusing others. For example, saying, 'I feel hurt when I'm not heard' is more constructive than, 'You never pay attention to me'.

Promote Active Listening

Active listening is a key component of effective conflict resolution. Encourage children to listen carefully to others' perspectives and show that they understand by summarising what they've heard. This helps ensure that everyone feels heard and validated, which is crucial for finding a resolution.

Teach Problem-Solving Techniques

Introduce children to problem-solving techniques that can help them address conflicts constructively. For example, teach them to identify the problem, brainstorm possible solutions, evaluate the pros and cons of each solution and choose the best course of action. This method helps children approach conflicts with a solution-oriented mindset.

Instil Compromise

Help children understand the importance of compromise in resolving conflicts. Teach them that finding a middle ground and making concessions is often necessary for reaching a resolution that is acceptable to everyone involved. Encourage them to be flexible and open to different solutions.

Use Positive Reinforcement

Acknowledge and praise children when they handle conflicts peacefully and use problem-solving skills effectively. Positive reinforcement encourages them to continue using these skills and reinforces their importance in maintaining healthy relationships. Positive reinforcement focuses on the desired action. For example, 'When you talked it out with your friend instead of arguing, I was really proud of you because it shows how well you can solve problems peacefully'.

Role-Playing and Other Activities to Encourage Problem-Solving

Role-playing and other interactive activities are valuable tools for teaching conflict resolution and problem-solving skills. These activities allow children to practise handling conflicts in a safe and controlled environment, helping them build confidence and competence.

Role-Playing Scenarios

Create role-playing scenarios that simulate common conflicts children might encounter. For example, role-play a situation where two friends want to play with the same toy and guide children through the process of resolving the conflict peacefully. Provide feedback and encouragement as they practise different approaches to finding a solution.

Conflict Resolution Games

Incorporate games and activities that focus on problem-solving and conflict resolution. For example, play 'The Negotiation Game', where children must work together to come up with a solution to a problem. These games make learning conflict resolution skills fun and engaging.

Group Discussions

Hold group discussions with family members about past conflicts and how they were resolved. Discuss what worked well and what could have been done differently. This reflection helps children understand the impact of different conflict resolution strategies and reinforces their learning.

How to Model Conflict Resolution as a Parent

Parents play a crucial role in teaching conflict resolution skills by modelling appropriate behaviour. Children learn by observing their parents' actions and reactions, so it's essential for parents to demonstrate effective conflict resolution techniques.

Stay Calm and Composed

When conflicts arise, model calmness and composure. Avoid raising your voice, using harsh language or becoming defensive. Instead, approach conflicts with a problem-solving mindset and a willingness to listen and understand others' perspectives.

Communicate Respectfully

Use respectful and constructive language when addressing conflicts. Show your children how to express feelings and needs without blame or accusation. For example, instead of saying, 'You never help with chores', try saying, 'I need help with chores, and I'd appreciate it if you could assist'.

Demonstrate Problem-Solving

Involve your children in problem-solving discussions and decisions. Show them how to evaluate different solutions and make choices based on mutual understanding and respect. This demonstrates how to approach conflicts with a focus on finding solutions rather than assigning blame.

Reflect on Conflicts

After resolving a conflict, reflect on the process with your children. Discuss what went well, what could be improved and how the resolution was achieved. This reflection reinforces the importance of effective conflict resolution and provides opportunities for learning and growth.

Teaching conflict resolution and problem-solving skills is essential for fostering a peaceful and supportive family environment. By encouraging open communication, active listening and compromise, and by using role-playing and other interactive activities, parents can help children develop the skills needed to handle conflicts constructively. Modelling effective conflict resolution as a parent further reinforces these skills and sets a positive example for children to follow. Through these efforts, families can build stronger, more resilient relationships and create a harmonious home environment.

In raising my two-year-old son, I recognise that conflicts can arise even in the simplest of situations, such as sharing toys with friends or expressing frustration over a favourite game. To teach him conflict resolution skills, I incorporate gentle guidance into our interactions. For instance, if he and another child both want the same toy, I step in and say, 'Let's take turns! You can play with it for a few minutes, and then it will be your friend's turn'.

I also emphasise the importance of using words to express feelings. When Daronn seems upset, I encourage him to say, 'I don't like that!' instead of crying. I explain that expressing his emotions helps others understand him better. I model how to resolve disagreements by verbally processing our interactions, saying things like, 'I understand you're frustrated.

How can we fix this together?'

Additionally, I use storytelling as a tool. I share simple stories where characters face conflicts and resolve them peacefully, prompting discussions on how they could handle similar situations. This not only reinforces the concept of conflict resolution but also allows him to think critically about solutions.

By consistently modelling these approaches, I aim to instil in Daronn a sense of agency and empathy when navigating conflicts, helping him grow into a child who can approach challenges with understanding and cooperation.

CHAPTER 11

DEVELOPING RESILIENCE IN CHILDREN

'It's your reaction to adversity, not the adversity itself, that shapes your character.'

– James Lane Allen, American novelist

Resilience is the capacity to bounce back from adversity, adapt to challenging situations and emerge stronger from life's difficulties. It's a critical trait that empowers individuals to handle stress, overcome setbacks and thrive despite challenges. For children, developing resilience can profoundly impact their ability to face life's ups and downs with confidence and perseverance. This chapter explores the importance of resilience, techniques to nurture it in children and how it contributes to a robust, supportive family environment.

Research from the American Psychological Association (2019) highlights that resilience is a vital component of mental health and emotional well-being. Children who exhibit resilience tend to have better academic performance, improved social skills and a lower incidence of mental health issues. The ability to adapt to challenges and recover from setbacks is linked to a supportive environment that fosters independence and encourages problem-solving. By teaching children to view challenges as opportunities for growth and development, parents play a crucial role in nurturing resilience. This foundation not only helps children navigate difficulties but also prepares them for future challenges, reinforcing their belief in their abilities.

What Resilience Is and Why It's Essential for Overcoming Adversity

Resilience is not an inherent trait but rather a skill that can be cultivated and strengthened over time. It involves the ability to manage stress, adapt to change and recover from setbacks. Resilient individuals are better equipped to handle challenges, maintain emotional stability and continue striving towards their goals despite obstacles.

Understanding Resilience

Resilience encompasses a range of qualities, including emotional regulation, problem-solving skills and a positive outlook. It enables individuals to face adversity with courage and determination, without being overwhelmed by stress or discouragement.

Importance for Overcoming Adversity

Children who develop resilience are better able to cope with stressors such as academic pressures, social challenges and family changes. They are more likely to persevere through difficulties, maintain a sense of hope and adapt their strategies when faced with setbacks.

Impact on Mental Health

Resilience is closely linked to mental health and well-being. Resilient children are less likely to experience anxiety, depression or other mental health issues. They have the tools to manage their emotions effectively and seek support when needed.

Techniques to Help Children Build Resilience in the Face of Challenges

Building resilience in children involves equipping them with the skills and mindset to navigate challenges effectively. Here are some techniques to help children develop resilience:

Foster a Growth Mindset

Promote the belief that abilities and intelligence can be developed through effort and learning. Encourage children to view challenges as opportunities for growth rather than insurmountable obstacles. Praise their efforts and perseverance, rather than just their achievements.

Support Emotional Expression

Create a safe space for children to express their feelings and emotions. Encourage them to talk about their experiences, fears and frustrations. Validate their emotions and provide comfort and support, helping them understand that it's okay to feel upset or frustrated.

Build Strong Relationships

Help children develop supportive relationships with family members, friends and mentors. Positive social connections provide a sense of belonging and security, which are crucial for resilience. Encourage children to seek support and build strong, trusting relationships with others.

Model Resilience

Demonstrate resilience in your own behaviour. Share your experiences of overcoming challenges and managing stress. Show children how to handle setbacks with a positive attitude and problem-solving approach. Your actions serve as a powerful example for them to follow.

Set Realistic Goals

Help children set achievable goals and develop a plan to reach them. Break larger goals into smaller, manageable tasks and celebrate their progress along the way. Setting and achieving goals builds confidence and reinforces the belief that they can overcome challenges.

How to Teach Children to View Failures as Opportunities for Growth

Failure is an inevitable part of life, and how children perceive and respond to it significantly impacts their resilience. Teaching children to view failures as opportunities for growth fosters a positive attitude and encourages persistence.

Reframe Failure

Help children reframe failure as a learning experience rather than a negative outcome. Encourage them to analyse what went wrong, identify lessons learned and consider how they can apply these lessons in the future. Emphasise that failure is a natural part of the learning process.

Encourage Risk-Taking

Create an environment where children feel safe to take risks and try new things. Support their efforts and encourage them to step out of their comfort zones. Praise their bravery and willingness to take on challenges, regardless of the outcome.

Focus on Effort and Improvement

Praise children for their effort and progress rather than just their successes. Highlight the value of persistence and hard work. Reinforce the idea that growth comes from continuous effort and learning, not just from achieving specific goals.

Normalise Setbacks

Help children understand that setbacks are a normal part of life and that everyone experiences them. Share stories of famous individuals or role models who have faced failures and setbacks but ultimately succeeded through perseverance and resilience.

The Role of Resilience in Creating a Strong, Supportive Family Unit

Resilience not only benefits individual children but also strengthens the overall family unit. A resilient family is better equipped to handle stress, support one another and maintain a positive and nurturing environment.

Enhancing Family Cohesion

When family members collectively embrace resilience, they support each other through challenges and work together to overcome difficulties. This collective strength fosters a sense of unity and reinforces the family's ability to handle adversity.

Building Emotional Strength

A resilient family provides a foundation of emotional support and stability. By modelling resilience and supporting each other, family members create a safe and nurturing environment that promotes emotional well-being and growth.

Developing Adaptive Coping Strategies

Resilient families develop adaptive coping strategies that help them navigate life's challenges. These strategies include effective communication, problem-solving and mutual support, which contribute to the family's overall resilience and ability to thrive.

Strengthening Family Bonds

Facing and overcoming challenges together strengthens family bonds and fosters a deeper sense of connection and trust. Resilient families view challenges as opportunities for growth and shared experiences, which enhances their relationships and overall family dynamic.

Developing resilience in children is a crucial component of fostering their ability to handle adversity and thrive despite challenges. By implementing techniques to build resilience, teaching children to view failures as opportunities for growth and modelling resilient behaviour, parents can equip their children with the skills and mindset needed to navigate life's difficulties. Additionally, a resilient family unit provides a supportive and nurturing environment that reinforces the importance of resilience and contributes to the overall well-being and strength of the family.

> In nurturing resilience in my two-year-old son, Daronn, I focus on creating a safe space where he can explore, make mistakes and learn. When he faces challenges like climbing to reach a toy or trying to stack blocks that keep falling, I encourage him to try again rather than immediately stepping in to help. I say, 'It's okay to fall! Just try again. I believe you can do it!' This promotes a growth mindset and reinforces the idea that setbacks are part of learning.
>
> Additionally, I model resilience in my own life. If I face a minor setback, such as spilling something while cooking, I express my feelings calmly and demonstrate how to clean it up. I might say, 'Oops! I made a mistake, but I can fix it.' This shows Daronn that making mistakes is a natural part of life and that handling them with grace is important.
>
> Storytelling is another effective tool I use. I share age-appropriate stories where characters face challenges and demonstrate resilience, encouraging Daronn to identify with them. I ask questions like, 'What would you do if you were in their shoes?' This prompts him to think critically about overcoming difficulties.
>
> Through these practices, I aim to equip Daronn with the skills to adapt and recover from life's challenges, fostering a resilient spirit that will serve him well as he grows.

CHAPTER 12

THE POWER OF POSITIVE REINFORCEMENT

'Behaviour is a mirror in which everyone displays his own image.'

– Johann Wolfgang von Goethe, German writer and statesman

Positive reinforcement is a powerful tool in shaping behaviour, boosting self-esteem and fostering a supportive family environment. By emphasising and rewarding desirable behaviours, parents can encourage children to repeat those behaviours and develop a sense of accomplishment and self-worth. This chapter explores the impact of positive reinforcement, strategies for effective praise and rewards, and how to balance it with discipline while avoiding the pitfalls of negative reinforcement.

Research conducted by the American Psychological Association (2018) indicates that positive reinforcement is significantly more effective than punishment in shaping desirable behaviours in children. By recognising and rewarding good behaviour, parents not only reinforce those actions but also enhance their child's self-esteem and motivation. Strategies such as specific praise, reward systems and celebrating small achievements create a supportive environment that fosters a child's sense of competence and belonging. Balancing positive reinforcement with appropriate limits ensures that children learn to navigate expectations without developing a reliance on external rewards, leading to internal motivation and a strong sense of self-worth.

The Impact of Positive Reinforcement on Behaviour and Self-Esteem

Positive reinforcement involves acknowledging and rewarding desired behaviours to increase their frequency. This approach not only motivates children to repeat those behaviours but also enhances their self-esteem and sense of achievement.

Reinforcing Desired Behaviours

When children receive positive reinforcement, they are more likely to repeat the behaviours that earned them praise or rewards. For example, praising a child for completing their homework on time encourages them to continue working diligently.

Boosting Self-Esteem

Positive reinforcement helps build a child's self-esteem by providing validation and recognition for their efforts. When children feel valued and appreciated, they develop a positive self-image and are more confident in their abilities.

Encouraging Motivation

Children are motivated to engage in behaviours that are recognised and rewarded. Positive reinforcement creates a sense of achievement and encourages children to strive for excellence, knowing their efforts will be acknowledged.

Strategies for Using Praise and Rewards to Encourage Good Behaviour

Effective use of praise and rewards involves more than just saying, 'Good job'. It requires thoughtful application and consistency to be truly effective.

Be Specific with Praise

Rather than offering generic praise, be specific about what the child did well. For example, instead of saying, 'Good job', try, 'I'm really impressed with how you organised your school materials and completed your homework without being reminded'. Specific praise helps children understand exactly what behaviours are being recognised.

Use Immediate Reinforcement

Provide praise or rewards as soon as possible after the desired behaviour occurs. Immediate reinforcement helps children make a clear connection between their actions and the positive outcome, reinforcing the behaviour more effectively.

Incorporate Various Rewards

Rewards can range from verbal praise to tangible items such as stickers or extra playtime. Tailor rewards to the child's preferences and the nature of the behaviour. For example, a child who loves reading might appreciate a new book as a reward for finishing their chores.

Encourage Effort and Improvement

Recognise and reward not just achievements but also effort and progress. Acknowledge when a child puts in extra effort or shows improvement in a challenging area. This approach encourages a growth mindset and reinforces the value of persistence and hard work.

Balancing Positive Reinforcement with Appropriate Discipline

While positive reinforcement is crucial, it's equally important to balance it with appropriate discipline to maintain a well-rounded approach to behaviour management.

Set Clear Expectations

Establish clear rules and expectations for behaviour so that children understand what is acceptable and what is not. Consistently apply these rules and use positive reinforcement to encourage adherence.

Implement Constructive Discipline

When discipline is necessary, ensure it is constructive and focused on teaching rather than punishment. For example, instead of harsh reprimands, explain the consequences of misbehaviour and involve the child in finding solutions to rectify the situation.

Avoid Over-Reliance on Rewards

While rewards are effective, avoid relying solely on them to motivate behaviour. Encourage intrinsic motivation by fostering a sense of personal responsibility and pride in doing the right thing, even without external rewards.

Maintain Consistency

Consistency is key in both positive reinforcement and discipline. Ensure that praise and rewards are given fairly and that disciplinary actions are applied consistently. Inconsistency can lead to confusion and undermine the effectiveness of both reinforcement and discipline.

How to Avoid the Pitfalls of Negative Reinforcement and Punishment

Negative reinforcement and punishment can have detrimental effects on behaviour and self-esteem if not managed carefully. Understanding and avoiding these pitfalls can enhance the effectiveness of positive reinforcement.

Understand Negative Reinforcement

Negative reinforcement involves removing an unpleasant stimulus in response to a desired behaviour. While it can increase behaviour, it may also create anxiety and stress. For instance, taking away a child's chores as a reward might lead to confusion about why the chores were initially given.

Avoid Harsh Punishment

Harsh punishment, such as yelling or physical discipline, can damage a child's self-esteem and create fear rather than understanding. Instead, focus on methods of discipline that teach and guide rather than punish.

Minimise Criticism

Frequent criticism or negative feedback can undermine a child's confidence and lead to resentment. Instead, balance criticism with positive reinforcement to ensure children feel valued and supported.

Use Consequences Wisely

When implementing consequences for undesirable behaviour, ensure they are reasonable, related to the behaviour and focused on teaching rather than simply penalising. For example, if a child refuses to do their homework, a consequence might be losing screen time but not a blanket punishment that affects their daily routine.

Promote Self-Regulation

Help children develop self-regulation skills by teaching them to understand their emotions and behaviours. Encouraging self-reflection and problem-solving can reduce the need for external discipline and foster internal motivation.

Emphasise Positive Outcomes

Shift the focus from avoiding negative outcomes to achieving positive results. By emphasising the benefits of good behaviour and the rewards that come from it, children are more likely to be motivated by positive reinforcement rather than fear of punishment.

Positive reinforcement is a powerful approach to shaping behaviour, enhancing self-esteem and creating a supportive family environment. By using specific, immediate praise and rewards, balancing reinforcement with appropriate discipline and avoiding the pitfalls of negative reinforcement and punishment, parents can effectively encourage desirable behaviours and foster a positive, nurturing atmosphere for their children.

> In raising my two-year-old son, Daronn, I actively implement positive reinforcement to encourage his good behaviour and develop his self-esteem. For instance, when Daronn finishes his meals or helps feed our dog, I make it a point to acknowledge his actions specifically. I might say, 'Daronn, I'm so proud of you for finishing your food! That shows you're growing strong!' or, 'Thank you for helping to feed Veerah! You're such a good helper!' This not only reinforces those behaviours but also boosts his confidence.
>
> In balancing discipline, I ensure that positive reinforcement is coupled with clear boundaries. If Daronn refuses to eat or throws his food in frustration, I calmly explain why that behaviour is not acceptable, reminding him of better ways to express his feelings. I then redirect his energy towards a more positive action, like using his words to ask for what he wants or helping set the table for our meal.
>
> By focusing on positive reinforcement, I aim to cultivate a nurturing environment where Daronn feels valued and motivated, laying the groundwork for healthy emotional development and self-regulation as he grows.

CHAPTER 13

THE ROLE OF COMMUNITY AND SUPPORT NETWORKS

'Alone, we can do so little; together, we can do so much.'

– Helen Keller

A supportive community and robust support networks play a pivotal role in raising children and fostering an environment where family violence is less likely to occur. Communities offer resources, role models and a sense of belonging that can significantly impact a child's development and well-being. This chapter explores the importance of community support, how to build a network of positive influences, the role of community engagement in preventing family violence and the benefits of encouraging children to contribute to and rely on their communities.

Research highlights the importance of community in fostering healthy child development and preventing family violence. A study by the National Institute of Justice emphasises that strong community ties can reduce the prevalence of violence by providing social support, resources and protective factors for families. Communities that engage in collective action and empower individuals create an environment where children feel secure and valued. When parents are supported by their community, they are better equipped to raise resilient children, and the likelihood of family violence decreases significantly. Building strong community connections promotes positive role models, facilitates open communication and enhances access to essential resources, all of which contribute to the well-being of families and individuals.

The Importance of a Supportive Community in Raising Children

A supportive community provides a safety net for families and children, offering emotional, social and practical support that enhances parenting and child development.

Emotional Support

Communities that offer emotional support can help parents navigate the challenges of raising children. Support groups, parenting workshops and social networks provide a space for sharing experiences, advice and encouragement. This collective support helps parents feel less isolated and more empowered.

Access to Resources

Communities often provide access to essential resources such as childcare, educational programs and health services. By leveraging these resources, parents can better support their child's growth and address any challenges they may face.

Socialisation Opportunities

Children benefit from interacting with diverse groups of people in their community. Socialisation opportunities through community events, sports and clubs help children develop social skills, build friendships and learn about different perspectives.

Building a Network of Positive Influences and Role Models

Creating a network of positive influences and role models is crucial for fostering a healthy environment for children. These individuals can provide guidance, support and inspiration, helping children develop positive traits and behaviours.

Identifying Role Models

Seek out individuals who embody the values and behaviours you want to instil in your children. These role models could be mentors, community leaders, educators or family members. Their actions and attitudes provide valuable examples for children to follow.

Encouraging Positive Relationships

Foster relationships with people who have a positive influence on your child's life. Encourage friendships with peers who demonstrate respect, kindness and integrity. These relationships contribute to a child's emotional and social development.

Building a Supportive Network

Develop a network of friends, family and community members who offer practical support and advice. This network can assist with childcare, provide emotional support and help navigate challenges. The presence of a supportive network strengthens the overall family unit and enhances resilience.

How Community Engagement Helps Prevent Family Violence

Community engagement is a key factor in preventing family violence by creating an environment of awareness, support and intervention.

Raising Awareness

Community programs and initiatives that focus on family violence education help raise awareness about the signs, consequences and resources available. Education fosters understanding and encourages individuals to seek help or offer support.

Providing Support Services

Communities can offer support services such as counselling, shelters and legal assistance for those affected by family violence. Access to these services ensures that individuals in need receive the help they require to escape abusive situations and rebuild their lives.

Promoting Prevention Programs

Engage in community prevention programs that address the root causes of family violence, such as unhealthy relationships and conflict resolution skills. These programs help individuals recognise and address harmful behaviours before they escalate.

Encouraging Reporting and Intervention

Communities should encourage reporting of family violence and provide clear pathways for intervention. By fostering a culture where violence is not tolerated and support is readily available, communities contribute to the prevention and reduction of family violence.

Encouraging Children to Contribute to and Rely on Their Communities

Teaching children to contribute to and rely on their communities instils a sense of responsibility and belonging while promoting positive social behaviours.

Involving Children in Community Activities

Encourage your children to participate in community events, volunteering opportunities and local organisations. Involvement helps children understand the importance of giving back and fosters a sense of connection to their community.

Teaching the Value of Contribution

Discuss with your children the benefits of contributing to their community, such as helping others, building relationships and creating a positive impact. Teach them that their actions, no matter how small, can make a difference.

Building Reliance on Support Networks

Help children recognise the value of relying on their community for support and guidance. Encourage them to seek help from trusted adults, mentors and friends when needed, and emphasise the importance of asking for support when facing challenges.

Fostering a Sense of Belonging

Create opportunities for children to develop strong connections within their community. A sense of belonging contributes to their emotional well-being and helps them feel valued and supported.

A supportive community and strong support networks are essential for raising children in a safe and nurturing environment. By building a network of positive influences, engaging in community initiatives to prevent family violence and encouraging children to contribute to and rely on their communities, parents can foster resilience, social responsibility and a sense of belonging. This collective effort creates a foundation where children can thrive and grow into responsible, compassionate individuals.

As a mother, I recognise the profound impact that community and support networks have on my son's development and overall well-being. To create a nurturing environment for him, I actively engage with our local community, which offers both resources and a sense of belonging.

For instance, I participate in parenting groups where we share experiences and advice on various aspects of raising children, including healthy communication and conflict resolution. These gatherings provide a platform for me to connect with other parents who share similar values, ensuring that my son grows up in an environment where respect and empathy are prioritised.

Additionally, I encourage my son to join local playgroups and activities that emphasise teamwork and collaboration. These experiences not only help him develop social skills but also teach him the importance of contributing to the community. By involving him in volunteer opportunities, such as helping at community gardens or participating in local clean-up days, I instil in him a sense of responsibility and the understanding that he is part of something larger.

When it comes to teaching resilience, I model how to approach challenges within our community. For example, if we encounter a problem – like a cancelled event or a change in plans – I guide him in brainstorming solutions and adapting to new situations. This not only builds his problem-solving skills but also strengthens his ability to navigate life's uncertainties.

By fostering strong community ties and involving my son in meaningful activities, I aim to create a supportive network around him. This approach not only enhances his emotional intelligence and resilience but also helps prevent the cycle of family violence, as he learns the value of connection, empathy and mutual support within a healthy community.

CHAPTER 14

HEALING FROM THE PAST AND MOVING FORWARD

'I can be changed by what happens to me. But I refuse to be reduced by it.'

– Maya Angelou

Addressing and healing from past traumas is essential for creating a positive and nurturing environment for children. The process of healing not only involves confronting and understanding past experiences but also actively working towards creating a healthier future. This chapter explores how families can address past traumas, the role of therapy and counselling, breaking free from negative cycles and moving forward with hope and resilience.

Addressing and Healing from Past Traumas within the Family

Acknowledging the Trauma

The first step in healing from past traumas is to acknowledge their existence. Whether it's personal trauma or familial experiences, recognising and accepting the impact of these events is crucial. This involves honest conversations about the past and its effects on the present.

Understanding the Impact

Traumas often leave lasting effects on individuals and families. Understanding how these experiences have shaped behaviours, relationships and emotional responses can provide insight into current challenges. This awareness is essential for addressing underlying issues and fostering healing.

Creating a Safe Space

To address past traumas, it's important to create a safe and supportive environment where family members feel comfortable discussing their experiences. This space should be free from judgment and focused on understanding and healing.

A cosy reading nook can be created in a corner filled with soft pillows, blankets and a variety of books. This space allows children to curl up with a book or journal their feelings in a quiet, comforting environment, making them feel secure and private.

Additionally, a family check-in space can be set up in the living room, featuring a comfortable area with a cosy blanket and a 'talking pillow' for children to hold when it's their turn to speak. This structured environment during family meetings fosters security and encourages open dialogue about their feelings.

Another option is an emotion board, which can be a wall or board where children can pin up drawings, pictures or words that represent their emotions. This visual representation enables children to express how they feel in a non-verbal way, sparking important discussions with caregivers about their emotions.

These spaces collectively help children feel safe and encouraged to express their feelings openly.

Practicing Self-Compassion

Healing from trauma involves practicing self-compassion. Family members should be gentle with themselves and each other, recognising that healing is a process that takes time and patience.

Self-compassion helps in coping with the emotional strain and fosters a positive outlook.

Let us look at a conversation that reflects the process of acknowledging grief and sharing feelings about the loss of a pet.

Child: Mum, I miss Max so much. I feel really sad.

Parent: I know, sweetie. Losing Max is really hard. Can you tell me what you miss the most about him?

Child: I miss playing with him and how he used to cuddle with me. Sometimes I feel like no one understands.

Parent: It's okay to feel that way. I miss him too. It's important to talk about how we feel. How about we remember some fun times we had with Max together?

Child: Yeah, I'd like that. It makes me feel better to remember the good times.

Parent: Let's look at some pictures and share our favourite memories. We can celebrate his life.

The Role of Therapy and Counselling in the Healing Process

Seeking Professional Help

Therapy and counselling play a significant role in the healing process. Professional therapists can provide guidance, support and strategies for addressing trauma. They offer a safe space for individuals to explore their feelings and work through complex emotions.

Family Therapy

Family therapy can be particularly beneficial in addressing collective trauma and improving family dynamics. It allows family members to express their feelings, understand each other's perspectives and work together towards healing and growth.

Developing Coping Strategies

Therapists can help families develop coping strategies to manage stress, anxiety and emotional challenges. These strategies may include mindfulness techniques, relaxation exercises and healthy communication practices.

Setting Goals for Healing

Therapy can assist families in setting achievable goals for healing. These goals may involve improving relationships, developing emotional resilience and creating a more supportive family environment.

Breaking Free from Negative Cycles to Create Positive Ones

Identifying Negative Patterns

Recognising and understanding negative cycles within the family is essential for breaking free from them. These patterns may include unhealthy communication, conflict avoidance or repeating harmful behaviours. Identifying these patterns helps in addressing the root causes.

Implementing Positive Changes

Once negative patterns are identified, families can work on implementing positive changes. This involves adopting healthier behaviours, improving communication and fostering supportive relationships. Positive changes contribute to breaking the cycle and creating a more nurturing environment.

Building New Habits

Creating positive cycles involves establishing new, healthier habits. Families can focus on practices such as regular family time, open communication and mutual support. Building these habits reinforces positive behaviour and strengthens family bonds.

Encouraging Growth and Development

Encouraging personal growth and development is key to creating positive change. Family members should support each other in pursuing personal goals, learning new skills and developing resilience. This collective growth fosters a positive family dynamic.

Moving Forward with Hope, Resilience and a Commitment to a Better Future

Embracing Hope

Hope is a powerful motivator for moving forward. Embracing hope involves focusing on the possibilities for a better future and believing in the potential for positive change. This optimistic outlook provides strength and encouragement during challenging times.

Building Resilience

Resilience is essential for overcoming obstacles and adapting to change. Families can build resilience by developing coping skills, fostering a supportive environment and maintaining a positive attitude. Resilience helps families navigate difficulties and emerge stronger.

To help kids develop coping skills, families can practise deep breathing exercises together to calm anxiety and stress. Encouraging journaling allows children to process their emotions, while teaching problem-solving skills helps them tackle challenges confidently. Incorporating positive affirmations and mindfulness activities, like meditation or yoga, promotes a positive mindset and emotional regulation.

Regular physical activity, such as walks or sports, can improve mood and reduce stress. Creating an environment of open communication fosters safe expression of feelings, and establishing daily routines provides stability during changes. Practicing gratitude shifts focus to positive aspects of life, and teaching kids that it's okay to seek support reinforces the importance of reaching out during tough times. By implementing these strategies, families can effectively help kids use coping skills and build resilience.

Committing to Growth

A commitment to growth involves continuously working towards personal and familial development. This commitment includes setting goals, addressing and celebrating achievements. It reflects a dedication to creating a better future and improving family dynamics.

Celebrating Progress

Recognising and celebrating progress is important for maintaining motivation and fostering a sense of accomplishment. Families should acknowledge their successes, no matter how small, and use them as a foundation for continued growth and improvement. Celebrating progress, whether it's mastering a new skill or overcoming a challenge, reinforces the idea that every step forward is worth acknowledging. Taking time to reflect on these successes not only boosts morale but also encourages everyone to keep striving for their goals.

Healing from past traumas and moving forward with hope and resilience is a transformative journey. By addressing past experiences, seeking therapy, breaking free from negative cycles and committing to positive change, families can create a nurturing and supportive environment for their children. This process not only fosters individual and familial growth but also sets the stage for a healthier, more fulfilling future.

As a mother, I am acutely aware of the importance of healing from past traumas, especially given my own experiences. I strive to create a safe and nurturing environment for my two-year-old son, Daronn, where he can thrive emotionally and socially. To do this, I practice open communication with him, which involves expressing my feelings in age-appropriate ways and encouraging him to do the same. For example, when he gets upset, I help him label his emotions – whether he is feeling sad, angry or frustrated. This practice not only fosters his emotional intelligence but also serves as a healing mechanism for me, allowing me to process my feelings constructively.

In addition, I prioritise routines and rituals that create a sense of stability for Daronn. We have family rituals, such as reading stories together at bedtime and sharing highlights of our day during dinner. These moments not only strengthen our bond but also serve as opportunities for me to model resilience and positivity, showcasing how we can embrace our past while looking forward to a brighter future.

Furthermore, I have sought therapy to work through my experiences, which has empowered me to break free from negative cycles. Through this journey, I learn coping strategies that I can share with Daronn, teaching him that it's okay to seek help and that vulnerability is a strength. By integrating these lessons into our daily lives, I am nurturing a foundation of healing and resilience, allowing Daronn to grow up in an environment where he feels safe, understood and empowered to express himself.

In our home, healing is a continuous process, and I am committed to modelling the behaviour I want to instil in him, ensuring that he knows that the past doesn't define his future.

CHAPTER 15

CREATING A LEGACY OF LOVE AND RESPECT

'They may forget what you said, but they will never forget how you made them feel.'

– Carl Buechner

Creating a legacy of love and respect is the culmination of a parent's efforts to instil positive traits in their children. This legacy is not only a reflection of the values imparted but also a powerful tool in breaking cycles of family violence and fostering a healthier, more compassionate future. In this chapter, we will explore the long-term impact of raising children with positive traits, how to pass on these values and the steps to build a lasting family legacy that contributes to eradicating family violence.

A journal article by Berkowitz and Bier (2005) discusses the significance of character education in fostering positive behaviours among children. It emphasises that children who grow up in nurturing environments, where values such as love, respect and empathy are consistently modelled, are more likely to develop strong moral compasses and engage in prosocial behaviour. The authors highlight that instilling these values can contribute to breaking the cycle of violence, as children who understand and embody respect and compassion are less likely to engage in harmful behaviours and more likely to promote positive relationships within their communities.

The Long-Term Impact of Raising Children with Positive Traits

Shaping Future Generations

Children who grow up with strong values of respect, empathy and resilience are more likely to carry these traits into adulthood. These qualities influence their interactions, relationships and decision-making, contributing to a more harmonious and supportive society. As these children become adults and parents themselves, they will model and pass on these values to their own children, perpetuating a cycle of positivity and respect.

Fostering Healthy Relationships

Positive traits such as empathy and respect are foundational for healthy relationships. Children raised with these values are more likely to develop strong, non-violent relationships throughout their lives. They learn to navigate conflicts constructively, support their partners and create nurturing environments for their families, thus contributing to the prevention of family violence.

Creating a Positive Ripple Effect

The impact of raising children with positive traits extends beyond the immediate family. These children often become role models in their communities, spreading the values they have learned and influencing others to adopt similar behaviours. This ripple effect can lead to broader societal changes, contributing to a culture of respect and kindness.

Ensuring Values of Respect, Empathy and Resilience Are Passed On

Modelling Behaviour

When a child sees their parent acting respectfully towards others, they will mimic that. Consistently modelling respect, empathy and resilience in daily interactions is crucial. Parents should demonstrate these values in their relationships, communication and problem-solving, providing a living example for their children to emulate.

Encouraging Open Dialogue

Maintaining open lines of communication allows children to discuss their thoughts, feelings and experiences. This dialogue provides opportunities to reinforce the importance of respect and empathy while addressing any questions or challenges they may face. Encouraging children to express themselves and listen to others fosters mutual understanding and respect.

Reinforcing Positive Behaviour

Positive reinforcement is essential in helping children internalise values. Acknowledge and praise respectful, empathetic and resilient behaviours to reinforce their importance. Constructive feedback should be provided in a supportive manner, guiding children towards continuous improvement and growth. When your child excitedly shares how they helped a friend who was feeling sad, you can respond by expressing your pride in their empathy, and if they mention struggling with homework, reassure them that it's okay to find it challenging and offer your support, reinforcing the importance of encouragement and growth.

Involving Children in Family Traditions

Family traditions and rituals can reinforce values and create a sense of belonging. Engaging children in activities that emphasise respect, empathy and resilience helps them internalise these values and understand their significance. Traditions such as family meetings, community service and storytelling can instil a deeper appreciation for these traits.

Family traditions and rituals can reinforce values and create a sense of belonging, but it's important to recognise that some children may not view these traditions positively and might choose to distance themselves as they grow older. To ensure that traditions are meaningful, families should engage children in discussions about their significance and encourage them to express their feelings. Involving children in activities that emphasise respect, empathy and resilience can help them internalise these values. By fostering an open environment where children feel heard, families can create traditions that resonate positively and are carried forward into their children's lives in a meaningful way.

Building a Family Legacy That Contributes to Eradicating Family Violence

Promoting Awareness and Education

Educating family members about family violence and its impact is essential for building a legacy of respect and safety. Providing information on healthy relationships, boundaries and conflict resolution helps create a family culture that actively works to prevent family violence.

Supporting Community Initiatives

Involvement in community initiatives that address family violence and support victims can extend the family's commitment to positive change. Volunteering, fundraising or participating in advocacy efforts can contribute to broader societal efforts to eradicate family violence and support affected individuals.

Continuously Reassessing Values and Practices

Building a lasting legacy requires ongoing reflection and adaptation. Regularly reassess family values and practices to ensure they align with the goal of fostering respect and empathy. Adapt strategies as needed to address new challenges and maintain a commitment to creating a positive family environment.

Final Thoughts and Encouragement for Parents

Creating a legacy of love and respect is a profound and rewarding endeavour. As parents, you have the power to shape the future by instilling values that will guide your children throughout their lives. Embrace the journey with dedication, knowing that your efforts are contributing to a more compassionate and respectful world.

Remember that the process of building this legacy is ongoing and dynamic. There will be challenges and setbacks, but each step taken towards fostering positive traits is a step towards a brighter future. Celebrate the progress, learn from the experiences and remain steadfast in your commitment to raising children who will carry forward the values of respect, empathy and resilience.

> In my journey as a mother, I have made it a priority to create a legacy of love and respect for my two-year-old son, Daronn. Understanding the importance of instilling these values, I consciously model behaviours that reflect compassion and kindness in our daily interactions. For instance, when we interact with others, whether it's greeting neighbours or visiting family, I encourage Daronn to use polite language, express gratitude and show appreciation for others. I often say, 'What do we say when someone gives us something?' to prompt him to respond with a heartfelt, 'Thank you!' This not only reinforces his understanding of respect but also demonstrates the importance of acknowledging others' efforts.
>
> Moreover, I incorporate storytelling into our routine, sharing tales that highlight the significance of empathy, respect and love. These stories often feature characters who face challenges but ultimately demonstrate kindness and understanding

towards others. After reading, I ask Daronn questions about the characters' feelings and decisions, which promotes his ability to empathise and reflect on the lessons learned.

Additionally, I emphasise the importance of nurturing relationships within our family. We frequently engage in activities together, such as cooking or playing games, where I encourage teamwork and cooperation. I highlight the value of respecting each other's ideas and preferences during these activities, teaching him that respect is a fundamental part of any relationship.

As I reflect on my past experiences and the values I want to instil in Daronn, I am committed to fostering an environment where love is freely expressed and respect is a guiding principle. By consciously cultivating this legacy, I hope to empower Daronn to grow into a compassionate individual who contributes positively to society, breaking the cycle of family violence and creating a better future for himself and those around him. Through our everyday actions, we are building a foundation that will carry forward through generations, instilling a legacy of love and respect that defines our family.

CHAPTER 16

THE ROLE OF COMMUNITIES IN SUPPORTING PARENTS AND RAISING RESILIENT CHILDREN

"Alone we can do so little; together we can do so much."

Helen Keller

A strong community can provide the social, emotional and practical resources that families need to thrive. By fostering an environment of mutual support, education and proactive engagement, communities can be instrumental in eradicating family violence and promoting the well-being of all members.

In their book *Infants and Children: Prenatal Through Middle Childhood*, Berk and Meyers (2016) emphasise the critical role that communities play in supporting parents and fostering resilience in children. They argue that strong community ties provide essential social and emotional resources, which are vital for families to thrive. The authors highlight how community engagement can enhance parenting practices, offering educational opportunities and mutual support that enable parents to share experiences and strategies. This collaborative approach not only helps parents navigate challenges but also creates a supportive environment for children, encouraging their emotional and social development. By fostering a sense of belonging and shared responsibility, communities can significantly contribute to the well-being and resilience of both parents and children, ultimately promoting healthier family dynamics and reducing the likelihood of family violence. This book discusses the importance of community support in child development, highlighting how strong community ties can enhance resilience in children and provide essential resources for families.

Building a Culture of Support and Safety

A resilient community begins with a shared commitment to the well-being of its members. Communities that prioritise safety, respect and support create an environment where families can flourish. This involves creating spaces where parents can connect, share experiences and access resources that help them raise their children in a positive, nurturing environment.

Local community centres, schools and religious institutions can serve as hubs for these efforts. By offering parenting classes, support groups and workshops on topics like emotional intelligence, conflict resolution and positive discipline, communities can empower parents with the tools they need to raise resilient children. These programs can also provide a platform for discussing the impact of family violence and strategies for preventing it.

Communities must also ensure that families have access to safe spaces where they can interact and build relationships. Parks, recreational facilities and community events offer opportunities for families to engage with one another in a supportive environment. These spaces not only provide a physical refuge but also foster social connections that are crucial for building resilience.

Moreover, communities can establish safe houses or crisis centres that offer immediate assistance to families experiencing family violence. These facilities should provide access to counselling, legal support and emergency shelter, ensuring that victims of family violence have a safe place to turn to in times of need.

Promoting Awareness and Education

Education is a powerful tool in the fight against family violence. Communities can play a pivotal role in raising awareness about the issue and educating members about the signs of abuse, the importance of healthy relationships and the resources available to those in need.

Community-wide campaigns, school programs and public service announcements can help normalise discussions about family violence and encourage individuals to speak out against it. By fostering a culture of awareness, communities can break the silence that often surrounds family violence and empower individuals to take action.

Supporting Parents Through Community Engagement

Communities that encourage active engagement among their members create a supportive network that can help parents navigate the challenges of raising children. Volunteering opportunities, neighbourhood watch programs and mentorship initiatives all contribute to a sense of collective responsibility for the well-being of the community's children.

Mentorship programs, in particular, can be highly effective in supporting parents. By pairing experienced parents with those who may be struggling, communities can provide guidance, advice and emotional support. This peer-to-peer model not only helps parents but also fosters a sense of solidarity and shared purpose.

Building Resilience through Collaboration

Ultimately, the strength of a community lies in its ability to collaborate and pool resources for the common good. Partnerships between local businesses, schools, healthcare providers and social services can create a comprehensive support system for families. For example, schools can work with local mental health professionals to offer counselling services to students and parents, while businesses can sponsor community events or provide financial support for local initiatives aimed at preventing family violence.

Collaboration also extends to law enforcement and local government. By working together, these entities can ensure that community policies and practices are aligned with the goal of creating a safe and supportive environment for families. This might include implementing community policing strategies, offering training for first responders on handling family violence cases or establishing neighbourhood outreach programs to connect families with the resources they need.

> As a parent, I recognise the importance of community in raising my two-year-old son. I actively engage with local parent groups and participate in community events, which not only allow me to connect with other families but also provide invaluable resources and support. For instance, when my son was beginning to explore his independence, I reached out to a parenting group for advice on fostering resilience and managing tantrums.
>
> Through this network, I learned practical strategies that I could implement at home, like setting consistent boundaries while encouraging self-expression. Additionally, I've noticed how other parents' experiences have shaped my approach, particularly in teaching my son empathy through playdates, where he interacts with peers and learns to share and cooperate.
>
> By fostering these connections, I am not only ensuring my son has a support system but also modelling the importance of community engagement. This approach reinforces the idea that we are all in this together, contributing to a nurturing environment where resilience can flourish.

CHAPTER 17

GOVERNMENT'S ROLE IN SUPPORTING FAMILIES AND ERADICATING FAMILY VIOLENCE

'To build a better future, we must ensure that our families have the resources they need to thrive. It is our collective responsibility to provide a safe and supportive environment for all.'

– **Barack Obama, former president of the United States of America**

While communities play a crucial role in supporting families, the government also has a significant responsibility in creating policies and providing resources that help parents raise resilient children and eradicate family violence. By enacting legislation, funding programs and promoting public awareness, the government can create a framework that supports families and ensures their safety and well-being.

In the article 'The Role of Government in Family Support', published in Journal of Family Issues, Kitzmann et al. (2016) discuss the essential role of government policies in providing support to families and preventing family violence. They argue that effective legislation and funding for family services, such as counselling, housing assistance and educational programs, can significantly impact family resilience and safety. The authors emphasise that public awareness campaigns are critical in changing societal attitudes towards family violence, thereby promoting a culture of safety and support for vulnerable families. They conclude that proactive government involvement is essential in creating a holistic framework that empowers families to thrive.

The federal government in Australia can support families by implementing legislation that protects victims of family violence, such as the *Family Violence Protection Act*, and by providing financial support for national programs like the *National Plan to Reduce Violence Against Women and their Children*. State governments play a crucial role by establishing local services, such as Family Relationship Centres, which offer mediation and support to families experiencing conflict, as well as funding training programs for educators and healthcare professionals to identify and address mental health issues in children.

At the local government level, community initiatives can include organising workshops and seminars on parenting skills and resilience-building, as well as developing community centres that provide access to support services and foster a sense of belonging. Public awareness campaigns, such as R U OK? Day, can promote conversations about mental health and encourage individuals to check in on friends and family members. Additionally, collaboration with non-profit organisations can enhance support for families by providing resources such as mental health counselling and family violence shelters. Together, these efforts create a comprehensive framework that ensures the safety and well-being of families in Australia.

Legislation and Policy Initiatives

One of the most important ways that the government can support families is through legislation that protects individuals from family violence and promotes the welfare of children. Laws that criminalise family violence, enforce restraining orders and provide protection for victims are essential in creating a society where families can feel safe and supported.

Anyone found to be a perpetrator of family violence should be required to participate in a comprehensive mandatory counselling program that includes individual therapy, group sessions focused on anger management and conflict resolution, education on healthy relationships and ongoing support to address underlying issues. This multifaceted approach is essential to effectively reduce the likelihood of repeat behaviour and promote lasting change.

Funding and Resources for Support Services

Government funding is essential for the operation of support services that assist families in need. Shelters, hotlines, counselling centres and legal aid organisations all rely on government support to provide their services. By allocating resources to these programs, the government ensures that families experiencing family violence have access to the help they need to escape abusive situations and rebuild their lives.

In addition to funding support services, the government can also invest in education and prevention programs. Public schools, for example, can be equipped with resources to teach students about healthy relationships, emotional regulation and conflict resolution. The Victorian government has one such program called Respectful Relationships, which is proving to be a success. These programs not only benefit children but also have a ripple effect on the wider community, as students bring the lessons they learn home to their families.

Public Awareness Campaigns

Raising public awareness about family violence is a key strategy in preventing it. Government-sponsored campaigns can help educate the public about the signs of family violence, the resources available to victims and the importance of supporting survivors. These campaigns can also challenge the societal norms and stereotypes that contribute to the perpetuation of violence.

By using various media platforms such as television, radio, social media and public service announcements, the government can reach a wide audience and create a culture of zero tolerance for family violence. Public awareness campaigns can also highlight the role of bystanders in preventing violence, encouraging individuals to speak out and take action if they witness abuse.

Support for Economic Stability

Economic instability is one of the factors that can exacerbate family violence. Governments can support families by implementing policies that promote economic stability, such as increasing the minimum wage, providing affordable childcare and offering job training programs. These measures can help reduce the financial stress that often contributes to family violence and empower individuals to leave abusive relationships.

Research in Australia has shown a clear connection between economic crises and family violence. A review by the Australian Institute of Criminology titled *The Impact of Economic Stress on Family Violence* highlights how economic stressors, such as unemployment and financial instability, can exacerbate tensions within households, leading to increased rates of family violence. Additionally, a study from the University of Melbourne, *Family Violence and Economic Abuse*, explores how economic abuse intertwines with family violence, particularly during economic downturns. It reveals that financial dependence can trap victims in abusive relationships, while economic stress may drive perpetrators to exert controlling behaviours. Together, these studies underscore the urgent need to address economic factors in efforts to prevent and respond to family violence in Australia.

Additionally, governments can provide financial support for survivors of family violence, such as housing assistance, emergency funds and access to healthcare. By ensuring that survivors have the resources they need to achieve financial independence, the government can help them break free from the cycle of violence and build a better future for themselves and their children.

Collaborating with Non-Governmental Organisations and Community Groups

Governments can enhance their efforts to support families and prevent family violence by collaborating with non-governmental organisations (NGOs) and community groups. These organisations often have the expertise, local knowledge and direct connections to the communities they serve, making them valuable partners in the fight against family violence.

The 2013 report by WHO *Global and regional estimates of violence against women: prevalence and health effects of intimate partner violence and non-partner sexual violence* discusses the importance of multi-sectoral approaches in addressing domestic violence, highlighting the effectiveness of partnerships between governments and NGOs in delivering targeted interventions. It emphasises that NGOs often have the local expertise and community connections necessary to create impactful programs tailored to specific populations, such as immigrant families or rural communities.

By working together, governments and NGOs can develop targeted programs that address the specific needs of different communities. This might include culturally sensitive services for immigrant families, specialised support for survivors of sexual violence or programs that focus on preventing violence in rural areas. Through these partnerships, the government can extend its reach and ensure that all families have access to the support they need.

As I navigate the challenges of raising my two-year-old son, I have seen firsthand how important government support can be for families like ours. For instance, when I sought parenting resources and workshops in our community, I discovered a local government initiative that offered free parenting classes. These classes provided me with valuable tools to foster resilience in my son and connect with other parents facing similar challenges. Additionally, when I applied for childcare subsidies, I was grateful for the assistance that allowed me to balance my responsibilities while ensuring that my son had access to quality early education. This experience highlighted how government programs not only empower parents but also help create a safer, more supportive environment for children to grow and thrive.

Helplines and Support Services (Australia)

Lifeline Australia

Phone: 13 11 14

Website: lifeline.org.au

Description: Provides 24/7 crisis support and suicide prevention services.

Kids Helpline

Phone: 1800 55 1800

Website: kidshelpline.com.au

A 24/7 counselling service for children and young people aged 5 to 25.

Beyond Blue

Phone: 1300 22 4636

Website: beyondblue.org.au

Provides support and resources for mental health issues, including anxiety and depression.

Headspace

Phone: 1800 650 890

Website: headspace.org.au

National youth mental health foundation providing early intervention services for 12-25-year-olds.

Australian Childhood Foundation

Phone: 1800 176 453

Website: childhood.org.au

Offers support for children affected by trauma, abuse, and neglect.

National Sexual Assault, Family Violence Counselling Service

Phone: 1800 737 732

Website: 1800respect.org.au

Provides support for people affected by sexual assault and family violence.

Mental Health Helpline (state-specific)

NSW: 1300 794 991

VIC: 1300 656 429

QLD: 1300 64 22 55

WA: 1300 555 788

SA: 1300 366 781

TAS: 1800 332 388

ACT: 02 6205 1065

State-specific mental health helplines providing support and resources.

SANE Australia

Phone: 1800 187 263

Website: https://www.sane.org

Provides information and support for people affected by mental illness.

Please note: The information provided in this resource guide is correct at the time of publication. For further information or assistance, please contact your healthcare provider or your local police.

Epilogue

As the journey through the pages of this book comes to a close, it is important to reflect on the profound impact that nurturing positive traits in children can have on breaking cycles of family violence and building resilient families. The principles discussed – empathy, respect, emotional intelligence and resilience – are not mere ideals but practical tools that can transform lives and create lasting change.

In the journey of parenting, the challenges may seem daunting, but each effort to instil these values is a step towards a brighter, more compassionate future. The lessons learned and the strategies employed are not just for today but for generations to come. By focusing on creating a safe, loving environment, fostering positive masculinity, empowering girls and promoting healthy communication, parents lay the groundwork for a world where family violence is no longer an issue.

The legacy of love and respect that you build within your family extends beyond your immediate circle. It influences your community, shapes societal norms and contributes to a culture of kindness and understanding. This book is a testament to the power of intentional parenting and the transformative potential of positive values.

As you move forward, remember that every small action counts and that the journey of raising children with positive traits is one of continuous growth and adaptation. Embrace the challenges with hope and resilience, knowing that your efforts are making a meaningful difference. The future holds promise and possibility, and by dedicating yourself to these principles, you are creating a legacy of love that will endure for generations.

I hope I have made the following message clear: the responsibility of raising resilient children and eradicating family violence does not rest on the shoulders of parents alone. It is a collective effort, one that requires the involvement of communities, governments and every individual who believes in a future where love, respect and empathy are the cornerstones of family life.

Throughout these pages, we have explored the multifaceted approaches needed to nurture strong, resilient families. We have discussed the importance of positive reinforcement, effective communication and conflict resolution in the home. We have examined the pivotal roles that communities and governments play in providing support, education and resources to families in need. And, perhaps most importantly, we have recognised that healing from past traumas and breaking negative cycles are essential steps towards building a brighter, more hopeful future.

As you reflect on the ideas and strategies presented in this book, I encourage you to take action no matter how small it may seem. Whether it's fostering open dialogue within your family, volunteering in your community or advocating for policy changes at the governmental level, every effort counts. Together, we can create a world where every child has the opportunity to grow up in a safe, loving, and resilient environment.

This book is more than just a guide; it is a call to action. It is an invitation to join a movement that seeks to create a legacy of love and respect, one that will endure for generations to come. Let us move forward with hope, courage and an unwavering commitment to making a difference in the lives of our children, our families and our communities. The future begins with us, and the time to act is now.

References

- World Health Organisation 2021, *Violence against women prevalence estimates 2018: global, regional and national prevalence estimates for intimate partner violence against women and global and regional prevalence estimates for non-partner sexual violence against women*, United Nations Inter-Agency Working Group on Violence Against Women Estimation and Data, Geneva

- World Health Organisation 2013, 'Global and regional estimates of violence against women: Prevalence and health effects of intimate partner violence and non-partner sexual violence', <https://www.who.int/reproductivehealth/publications/violence/9789241564625/en/>

- Harvard University 2015, 'The science of resilience: How to build a strong foundation for children', Harvard Centre on the Developing Child, <https://developingchild.harvard.edu/resources/>

- Ekman, P 2003, *Emotions revealed: Recognising faces and feelings to improve communication and emotional life*, Times Books/Henry Holt and Co

- Goleman, D 1995, *Emotional intelligence: Why it can matter more than IQ*, Bantam Books.

- Lickona, T 1991, *Educating for character: How our schools can teach respect and responsibility*, Bantam Books.

- Brooks, R, & Goldstein, S 2001, *Raising resilient children: Fostering strength, hope, and resilience in your child*, McGraw-Hill.

- Kimmel, M 2008, *Guyland: The perilous world where boys become men*, HarperCollins.

- Hinkelman, L 2013, *Girls Without Limits: Helping girls succeed in relationships, academics, careers, and life*, Jossey-Bass.

- Gottman, J 1997, *The Seven Principles for Making Marriage Work*, Crown Publishers.

- Espelage, D. L, Low, S, & De La Rue, L 2012, 'Relations between peer victimisation subtypes, family violence, and psychological outcomes during early adolescence', *Psychology of Violence*, vol. 2, no. 4, pp. 313–324, <https://doi.org/10.1037/a0027386>

- American Psychological Association 2019, 'The road to resilience', <https://www.apa.org/helpcenter/road-resilience>

- American Psychological Association 2018, 'The impact of positive reinforcement on behaviour and self-esteem', <https://www.apa.org/topics/positive-reinforcement>

- Berkowitz, M. W, & Bier, M. C 2005, 'Character education: A shared responsibility', *The Educational Forum*, vol 69, no. 2, pp. 175-185, <https://doi.org/10.1080/00131720508984692>

- Kitzmann, K. M, Gaylord-Harden, N. K, Dempsey, J, & Prioleau, T 2016, 'The role of government in family support', *Journal of Family Issues*, vol. 37, no. 7, pp. 925-948, <https://doi.org/10.1177/0192513X15579422>

Acknowledgements

To My Publisher

I would like to extend my heartfelt gratitude to the entire team at Busybird Publishing for making *Raising Resilient Families* possible.

A special thanks to Kev Howlett, the owner, head honcho and studio manager, for your unwavering support and vision.

Thank you to Les Zigomanis and the production team for your expertise and dedication throughout this journey.

Lastly, I want to express my deepest appreciation to my editor and guide, Anna B, who travelled every chapter with me, offering invaluable insights and encouragement.

Together, you have all played an essential role in bringing this project to life.

To My Readers

I would also like to extend my heartfelt gratitude to all the readers of *Raising Resilient Families*. Your support and engagement mean the world to me. It is my hope that this book resonates with you and serves as a valuable resource in your journey towards raising resilient children and fostering a compassionate community. Thank you for being a part of this journey, and I look forward to hearing your thoughts and experiences!

About the Author

Deborah Sugirthakumar, an Australian Tamil, was born during the Sri Lankan civil war, where survival was a daily challenge. Migrating to Australia in her early childhood, her family embraced a new life of resilience and hope. Deborah holds a degree in health science from Deakin University and completed the Early Childhood Language Program at Melbourne University. Recently, she completed her studies from Monash University with a focus on education, aspiring to pursue a career as an educator.

Deborah has built a diverse professional background in public service, and she currently serves as the Secretary of WYN FM Radio Station. She co-produces the Tamil language show *Vaanisai* and also produces her own English language show, *Mindful Moments*, which addresses crucial issues and empowers listeners. Additionally, she contributes to the local newspaper on these topics.

Her personal experiences have fuelled her advocacy for family violence awareness and mental health resilience. As a mother, Deborah is committed to raising her son with values of empathy, responsibility and respect. Through her work, she strives to inspire positive change and help others find strength and hope in the face of adversity.

www.ingramcontent.com/pod-product-compliance
Lightning Source LLC
Chambersburg PA
CBHW041146110526
44590CB00027B/4140